WINDOWS 3.1
FOR
DUMMIES™

Quick
Reference

by Greg Harvey

IDG
BOOKS

IDG Books Worldwide, Inc.
An International Data Group Company

Foster City, CA ♦ Chicago, IL ♦ Indianapolis, IN ♦ Braintree, MA ♦ Dallas, TX

Windows™ 3.1 For Dummies® Quick Reference, 2nd Edition

Published by
IDG Books Worldwide, Inc.
An International Data Group Company
919 E. Hillsdale Blvd.
Suite 400
Foster City, CA 94404

Library of Congress Catalog Card No.: 94-77187

ISBN: 1-56884-951-6

Printed in the United States of America

10 9 8 7 6 5

2D/SY/QT/ZV

Distributed in the United States by IDG Books Worldwide, Inc.

Distributed by Macmillan Canada for Canada; by Computer and Technical Books for the Caribbean Basin; by Contemporanea de Ediciones for Venezuela; by Distribuidora Cuspide for Argentina; by CITEC for Brazil; by Ediciones ZETA S.C.R. Ltda. for Peru; by Editorial Limusa SA for Mexico; by Transworld Publishers Limited in the United Kingdom and Europe; by Al-Maiman Publishers & Distributors for Saudi Arabia; by Simron Pty. Ltd. for South Africa; by IDG Communications (HK) Ltd. for Hong Kong; by Toppan Company Ltd. for Japan; by Addison Wesley Publishing Company for Korea; by Longman Singapore Publishers Ltd. for Singapore, Malaysia, Thailand and Indonesia; by Unalis Corporation for Taiwan; by WS Computer Publishing Company, Inc. for the Philippines; by WoodsLane Pty. Ltd. for Australia; by WoodsLane Enterprises Ltd. for New Zealand.

For general information on IDG Books in the U.S., including information on discounts and premiums, contact IDG Books at 800-434-3422 or 415-655-3000.

For information on where to purchase IDG Books outside the U.S., contact IDG Books International at 415-655-3021 or fax 415-655-3295.

For information on translations, contact Marc Jeffrey Mikulich, Director, Foreign & Subsidiary Rights, at IDG Books Worldwide, 415-655-3018 or fax 415-655-3295.

For sales inquiries and special prices for bulk quantities, write to the address above or call IDG Books Worldwide at 415-655-3000.

For information on using IDG Books in the classroom, or ordering examination copies, contact Jim Kelly at 800-434-2086.

is a registered trademark under exclusive license to IDG Books Worldwide, Inc., from International Data Group, Inc.

About the Author

Greg Harvey, the author of over 30 computer books, has been training business people in the use of IBM PC, DOS, and software application programs such as WordPerfect, Lotus 1-2-3, and dBASE since 1983. He has written numerous training manuals, user guides, and books for business users of software. He currently teaches Lotus 1-2-3 and dBASE courses in the Department of Information Systems at Golden Gate University in San Francisco. Harvey is the author of *Excel For Dummies, 1-2-3 For Dummies, PC World WordPerfect 6 Handbook, DOS For Dummies Quick Reference,* and *WordPerfect For Dummies Quick Reference,* all from IDG Books.

ABOUT IDG BOOKS WORLDWIDE

Welcome to the world of IDG Books Worldwide.

IDG Books Worldwide, Inc., is a subsidiary of International Data Group, the world's largest publisher of computer-related information and the leading global provider of information services on information technology. IDG was founded more than 25 years ago and now employs more than 7,200 people worldwide. IDG publishes more than 233 computer publications in 65 countries (see listing below). More than fifty million people read one or more IDG publications each month.

Launched in 1990, IDG Books Worldwide is today the #1 publisher of best-selling computer books in the United States. We are proud to have received 3 awards from the Computer Press Association in recognition of editorial excellence, and our best-selling ...For Dummies™ series has more than 12 million copies in print with translations in 25 languages. IDG Books, through a recent joint venture with IDG's Hi-Tech Beijing, became the first U.S. publisher to publish a computer book in the People's Republic of China. In record time, IDG Books has become the first choice for millions of readers around the world who want to learn how to better manage their businesses.

Our mission is simple: Every IDG book is designed to bring extra value and skill-building instructions to the reader. Our books are written by experts who understand and care about our readers. The knowledge base of our editorial staff comes from years of experience in publishing, education, and journalism — experience which we use to produce books for the '90s. In short, we care about books, so we attract the best people. We devote special attention to details such as audience, interior design, use of icons, and illustrations. And because we use an efficient process of authoring, editing, and desktop publishing our books electronically, we can spend more time ensuring superior content and spend less time on the technicalities of making books.

You can count on our commitment to deliver high-quality books at competitive prices on topics consumers want to read about. At IDG, we value quality, and we have been delivering quality for more than 25 years. You'll find no better book on a subject than an IDG book.

John J. Kilcullen

John Kilcullen
President and CEO
IDG Books Worldwide, Inc.

WINNER
Eighth Annual
Computer Press
Awards ≧ 1992

WINNER
Ninth Annual
Computer Press
Awards ≧ 1993

IDG Books Worldwide, Inc., is a subsidiary of International Data Group, the world's largest publisher of computer-related information and the leading global provider of information services on information technology. International Data Group publishes over 220 computer publications in 65 countries. More than fifty million people read one or more International Data Group publications each month. The officers are Patrick J. McGovern, Founder and Board Chairman; Kelly Conlin, President; Jim Casella, Chief Operating Officer. International Data Group's publications include: ARGENTINA'S Computerworld Argentina, Infoworld Argentina; AUSTRALIA'S Computerworld Australia, Computer Living, Australian PC World, Australian Macworld, Network World, Mobile Business Australia, Publish!, Reseller, IDG Sources; AUSTRIA'S Computerwelt Oesterreich, PC Test; BELGIUM'S Data News (CW); BOLIVIA'S Computerworld; BRAZIL'S Computerworld, Connections, Game Power, Mundo Unix, PC World, Publish, Super Game; BULGARIA'S Computerworld Bulgaria, PC & Mac World Bulgaria, Network World Bulgaria; CANADA'S CIO Canada, Computerworld Canada, InfoCanada, Network World Canada, Reseller; CHILE'S Computerworld Chile, Informatica; COLOMBIA'S Computerworld Colombia, PC World; COSTA RICA'S PC World; CZECH REPUBLIC'S Computerworld, Elektronika, PC World; DENMARK'S Communications World, Computerworld Danmark, Computerworld Focus, Macintosh Produktkatalog, Macworld Danmark, PC World Danmark, PC Produktguide, Tech World, Windows World; ECUADOR'S PC World Ecuador; EGYPT'S Computerworld (CW) Middle East, PC World Middle East; FINLAND'S MikroPC, Tietoviikko, Tietoverkko; FRANCE'S Distributique, GOLDEN MAC, InfoPC, Le Guide du Monde Informatique, Le Monde Informatique, Telecoms & Reseaux; GERMANY'S Computerwoche, Computerwoche Focus, Computerwoche Extra, Electronic Entertainment, Gamepro, Information Management, Macwelt, Netzwelt, PC Welt, Publish, Publish; GREECE'S Publish & Macworld; HONG KONG'S Computerworld Hong Kong, PC World Hong Kong; HUNGARY'S Computerworld SZT, PC World; INDIA'S Computers & Communications; INDONESIA'S Info Komputer; IRELAND'S ComputerScope; ISRAEL'S Beyond Windows, Computerworld Israel, Multimedia, PC World Israel; ITALY'S Computerworld Italia, Lotus Magazine, Macworld Italia, Networking Italia, PC Shopping Italy, PC World Italia; JAPAN'S Computerworld Today, Information Systems World, Macworld Japan, Nikkei Personal Computing, SunWorld Japan, Windows World; KENYA'S East African Computer News; KOREA'S Computerworld Korea, Macworld Korea, PC World Korea; LATIN AMERICA'S GamePro; MALAYSIA'S Computerworld Malaysia, PC World Malaysia; MEXICO'S Compu Edicion, Compu Manufactura, Computacion/Punto de Venta, Computerworld Mexico, MacWorld, Mundo Unix, PC World, Windows; THE NETHERLANDS'S Computer! Totaal, Computable (CW), LAN Magazine, Lotus Magazine, MacWorld; NEW ZEALAND'S Computer Buyer, Computerworld New Zealand, Network World, New Zealand PC World, Network World; NIGERIA'S PC World Africa; NORWAY'S Computerworld Norge, Lotusworld Norge, Macworld Norge, Maxi Data, Networld, PC World Ekspress, PC World Nettverk, PC World Norge, PC World's Produktguide, Publish&r Multimedia World, Student Data, Unix World, Windowsworld; PAKISTAN'S PC World Pakistan; PANAMA'S PC World Panama; PERU'S Computerworld Peru, PC World; PEOPLE'S REPUBLIC OF CHINA'S China Computerworld, China Infoworld, China PC Info Magazine, Computer Fan, PC World China, Electronics International, Electronics Today/Multimedia World, Electronic Product World, China Network World, Software World Magazine, Telecom Product World; PHILIPPINES' Computerworld Philippines, PC Digest (PCW); POLAND'S Computerworld Poland, Computerworld Special Report, Networld, PC World/Komputer, Sunworld; PORTUGAL'S Cerebro/PC World, Correio Informatico/Computerworld, MacIn; ROMANIA'S Computerworld, PC World, Telecom Romania; RUSSIA'S Computerworld-Moscow, Mir - PK (PCW), Sety (Networks); SINGAPORE'S Computerworld Southeast Asia, PC World Singapore; SLOVENIA'S Monitor Magazine; SOUTH AFRICA'S Computer Mail (CIO),Computing S.A.,Network World S.A., Software World; SPAIN'S Advanced Systems, Amiga World, Computerworld Espana, Communicaciones World, Macworld Espana, NeXTWORLD, Super Juegos Magazine (GamePro), PC World Espana, Publish; SWEDEN'S Attack, ComputerSweden, Corporate Computing, Macworld, Mikrodatorn, Natverk & Kommunikation, PC World, CAP & Design, Datalngenjoren, Maxi Data,Windows World; SWITZERLAND'S Computerworld Schweiz, Macworld Schweiz, PC Tip; TAIWAN'S Computerworld Taiwan, PC World Taiwan; THAILAND'S Thai Computerworld; TURKEY'S Computerworld Monitor, Macworld Turkiye, PC World Turkiye; UKRAINE'S Computerworld, Computers+Software Magazine; UNITED KINGDOM'S Computing /Computerworld, Connexion/Network World, Lotus Magazine, Macworld, Open Computing/Sunworld; UNITED STATES' Advanced Systems, AmigaWorld, Cable in the Classroom, CD Review, CIO, Computerworld, Computerworld Client/Server Journal, Digital Video, DOS World, Electronic Entertainment Magazine (E2), Federal Computer Week, Game Hits, GamePro, IDG Books, Infoworld, Laser Event, Macworld, Maximize, Multimedia World, Network World, PC Letter, PC World, Publish, SWATPro, Video Event; URUGUAY'S PC World Uruguay; VENEZUELA'S Computerworld Venezuela, PC World; VIETNAM'S World Vietnam. 2/27/95

Acknowledgments

A very special thank you to Victor Robert Garza, who pulled the text and figures together for this book. Bob is a Test Development Specialist for *InfoWorld* Magazine. He took time from his busy schedule of work and graduate studies (not to mention boogie boarding and rollerblading) to make this book happen on time.

I want to thank the following people, as well, who worked so hard to make this book a reality:

David Solomon and John Kilcullen for their support for this "baby" Dummies book.

Brandon Nordin and Milissa Koloski for coming up with the original concept of quick references for the rest of us.

Janna Custer and Megg Bonar for straightening out all the contract details.

Diane Steele, Tracy Barr, Sandy Blackthorn, and Julie King for their editorial assistance.

Michael Partington for the tech review and Beth Jenkins and the layout folks in Production.

Last, but never least, I want to acknowledge my indebtedness to Dan Gookin, whose vision, sardonic wit, and (sometimes) good humor produced *DOS For Dummies*, the "Mother" of all Dummies books. Thanks for the inspiration and the book that made it all possible, Dan.

Greg Harvey
Inverness, California

(The publisher would like to give special thanks to Patrick J. McGovern, without whom this book would not have been possible.)

Credits

Executive Vice President, Strategic Product Planning and Research
David Solomon

Editorial Director
Diane Graves Steele

Acquisitions Editors
Megg Bonar
Janna Custer

Brand Manager
Judith A. Taylor

Editorial Managers
Tracy L. Barr
Sandra Blackthorn

Editorial Assistants
Tamara S. Castleman
Stacey Holden Prince
Elizabeth H. Reynolds
Kevin Spencer

Acquisitions Assistant
Suki Gear

Production Director
Beth Jenkins

Associate Project Coordinator
Valery Bourke

Pre-Press Coordinators
Tony Augsburger
Steve Peake

Project Editor
Julie King

Technical Reviewers
Michael Partington
Tim Stanley

Production Staff
Sherry Dickinson Gomoll
Laura Puranen
Dwight Ramsey

Proofreader
Charles A. Hutchinson

Indexer
Steve Rath

Contents at a Glance

Introduction

Welcome to the *Windows 3.1 For Dummies Quick Reference,* a quick reference that looks at the lighter side of Windows features and tasks (such as it is). This book not only gives you the lowdown on Windows, it also rates each task with icons indicating how likely you are to get involved with a particular activity as well as your general safety if you do so (see the "The cast of icons" later in this introduction for a sneak preview).

For your convenience, this book is divided into seven sections. Each Windows feature and task is handled in a similar way. Below the name, replete with its suitability and safety icons, you'll find a brief description of the function. If this description reads like stereo instructions, recheck the suitability icon: You may be out of your league.

Below the description comes the "Steps" section. Here, you find the "more answers, less reading" part of this book. You can follow the steps you need to take to accomplish a Windows task or learn about Windows parts in a "picturesque" sequence.

Following the "Steps" section, in most cases, you'll find detailed explanations of options and features.

Bringing up the rear, you'll find a "More stuff" section where I stick in any tips, warnings, reminders, or other trivia that just might come in handy while you're roaming around this area of Windows.

This book is designed for beginners who have at least some experience with Windows but are still unsure about what's going on. If you are really a greenhorn when it comes to Windows, please get your hands on a copy of Andy Rathbone's excellent *Windows 3.1 For Dummies,* 2nd Edition and *MORE Windows For Dummies.* These two books are much more extensive references and provide a good starting point for learning about Windows.

To make it easier for you to go back and forth between the more telegraphic information presented in this quick reference and *Windows 3.1 For Dummies,* 2nd Edition and *MORE Windows For Dummies,* I've cross-referenced many topics to related discussions in those books. (Look for the Cross Reference icons.)

How do I use this book?

You've all heard of on-line help. Well, just think of this book as onside help. Keep it by your side when you're at the computer, and, *before* you try to perform a Windows task that you're the least bit unsure of, look it up in the appropriate section. Scan the entry, looking for any warnings (those bomb icons). Follow the steps to guide you through the options.

The cast of icons

In your travels through this book, you'll come across the following icons:

Recommended for your average Windows user.

Not recommended for your average Windows user.

Not suitable for your average Windows user, but you may get stuck having to use this feature anyway.

Safe for your data.

Generally safe in most circumstances unless you really don't follow instructions; then look out!

Potentially dangerous to data but necessary in the scheme of things. Be very careful with this task. Better yet, get somebody else to do it for you.

Safe only in the hands of a programmer or some other totally techy person. Stay clear unless they let you sign a release form and give you hazard pay.

A tip to make you a more clever Windows user.

Look out! There's some little something in this task that can get you into trouble (even when it's rated safe or generally safe).

Just a little note to remind you of some trivia or other that may someday save your bacon.

A handy-dandy guide to point you straight to the sections in *Windows 3.1 For Dummies*, 2nd Edition and *MORE Windows For Dummies* where you can find more examples of how to use this command.

A pointer to another related feature or task in this book.

Part 1:
Windows Basics

Control Menu

Short menu of commands attached to every window.

The control menu contains a number of commands like Move and Size (which are most often accessed with the mouse) and Close (Ctrl+F4) that are especially useful when you aren't into using the mouse. To display the control menu, simply click the window's control menu button (the square button in the upper left corner with the small bar in its middle — the one that kinda looks like a file cabinet drawer.) After making new selections in a control menu, press the Enter key to put them into effect. To close a control menu without making changes, press the Esc key twice.

Steps

❶

❷

Restore	
Move	
Size	
Minimize	
Maximize	
Close	Ctrl+F4
Next	Ctrl+F6

Common Options	What They Do
Restore	This command restores — hence the name — a maximized or minimized window back to a reasonable size.
	Pressing Alt, the spacebar, and R also restores a window. This command is grayed out unless the window is maximized.
Move	It's usually easier just to click and drag on a window's title bar with the mouse to move a window.
	If you're stuck with just the keyboard, pressing Alt, the spacebar, and M begins the moving process. The arrow changes to a cross, and the outline of the window changes colors. Using one of the arrow keys, move the window to the desired location. Once you start moving a window, the cross changes back to an arrow. Press Enter when you are done moving the window.

Common Options	What They Do
	If you change your mind while moving the window, press Esc and the window will return to its original position.
Size	Very similar to moving a window, except that this command allows you to change the vertical or horizontal size of the window with the arrow keys.
	Pressing Alt, the spacebar, and S starts the resizing process. If only it were that easy for the waistline...
Minimize	This command causes a window to shrink to a little icon at the bottom of the screen (see "Icons" later in Part I if you don't know an icon from an ice cube). Pressing Alt, the spacebar, and N also minimizes a window.
Maximize	This command causes a window to fill up the entire screen. Pressing Alt, the spacebar, and X also maximizes a window.
Close (Ctrl+F4)	This command closes a window. An easier way to close a window, however, is by double-clicking the control menu button — the same button you clicked once to open the control menu.
Next	Usually found in a word processing application, this command lets you switch between an open document window and an icon representing another document.
Switch To... (Ctrl+Esc)	This command name is followed by an ellipsis (...); choosing this command name displays the Task List box. The Task List box keeps track of all the programs you have open and lets you switch between the programs quickly.
	The Task List box has command buttons along the bottom that offer you various options for operations you can perform on the selected open program (see "Dialog Boxes" later in Part I if you don't know a command button from a cotton gin).
	You can also get to the Task List box by double-clicking anywhere on the Windows desktop or background, called the *wallpaper*.

See the example in *Windows 3.1 For Dummies,* 2nd Edition, Chapter 6, "The Dopey Control-Menu Box." Also, see the example in *Windows 3.1 For Dummies*, 2nd Edition, Chapter 7, "The Way-Cool Task List," and the example in *MORE Windows 3.1 For Dummies*, Chapter 1, "Finding a Misplaced Window."

More stuff

By giving the control menu button a swift double-click, you can easily exit from any window.

You can minimize and maximize windows quickly by clicking the buttons on the far right side of the title bar; use the down-arrow button to minimize and the up-arrow button to maximize.

When a command name is dimmed, you know that the command is temporarily off-limits.

When you're running DOS programs like WordPerfect for DOS in Windows, the control menu button has the additional commands Edit, Settings, and Fonts (see "Changing the Settings for Running a Non-Windows Application" in Part II, or "MS-DOS Prompt" in Part III, for explanations of these commands).

To switch quickly to a different program that is running on your desktop, hold down the Alt key and then press the Tab key repeatedly to switch between applications. When you switch to the one you want, let go of the Alt key to run that application (Windows 3.1 only).

Dialog Boxes

Universally used in Windows and Windows programs to give you more menu choices or to alert you to a problem in the making. After making new selections in a dialog box, choose the OK button to put them into effect. To close a dialog box without making changes, press Esc or choose the Cancel button.

Radio buttons   Text boxes   Command buttons

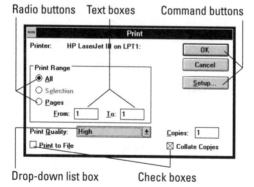

Drop-down list box   Check boxes

Dialog Boxes 7

List box

Parts of a Dialog Box	What You Do with Them
Text box	Let's say that you type in a new setting or edit the current setting that appears in the box. In an empty box, you see a flashing vertical bar called an *insertion point.* When you enter stuff from the keyboard, the insertion point moves to the right, depositing characters along the way.
	If the text inside the box is selected, anything you type replaces the highlighted text. You can also delete highlighted text by just pressing the Delete or Backspace key.
List box	Displays an alphabetical list of all choices for an item.
	Use the scroll bar on the right to display new choices (see "Parts of a Window" later in Part I for an explanation of scroll bars). The current choice is highlighted in the list.
Drop-down list box	Looks like a text box with a down-arrow button right next door.
	Click the arrow button to open a list box of possible choices. If there are more choices than will fit in the box, use the scroll bar on the right to display more choices.
Radio (option) button	Used with items that allow you to choose only one of several options. The selected option appears with a dot in the middle of the radio button and a faint dotted line around the option name.

(continues)

Parts of a Dialog Box	What You Do with Them
Check box	Used with items that allow you to choose more than one option. Selected options appear with X inside the box, while the current check box option appears with a faint dotted line around the option name.
Command button	Used to initiate an action such as putting the options you've selected into effect with the OK button.
	If the command name is followed by an ellipsis (...), choosing the button displays another dialog box. If the command name is followed by two greater-than symbols (>>), choosing the button expands the current dialog box to display more choices. If the command name is dimmed, the button is temporarily off-limits.

To select an item in a dialog box, simply click it with the mouse. If you're not into using the mouse and need a quick reminder of the keystroke shortcuts for getting around a dialog box and selecting items, see Part VII, "Keystroke Shortcuts in Windows."

Keep in mind that you can always move a dialog box to a new part of the screen by dragging it around by its little title bar (see "Parts of a Window" later in Part I if you don't know a title bar from a title page). Just because you can move a dialog box like other standard windows, don't get it in your head that you can resize dialog boxes like you do program and document windows. Dialog boxes don't ever change size unless you choose a Command button with >> at the end of its name, which tends to puff them up a bit.

See the example in *Windows 3.1 For Dummies*, 2nd Edition, Chapter 6, "Dialog Box Stuff (Lots of Gibberish)."

More stuff

You know that a dialog box is about to appear in your life whenever you see a pull-down menu command in Windows or a Windows program that is followed by an ellipsis (that's Greek for three dots in a row). For example, you know that choosing the

New... command on the File menu in the Windows Program
Manager displays a dialog box because the command name
appears as New... rather than simply New (no ellipsis) on the File
pull-down menu.

Icons

Small pictures that you choose to make Windows or a Windows
program do things you want them to do — like start a program or
print a file.

To choose an icon with the mouse, position the mouse pointer on
it and click. When dealing with a program-item, application, or
group icon in the Program Manager or a directory, program file,
or document file icon in the File Manager (see tables below), you
double-click the icon when you want to open it (you can alternatively click the icon to select it and then press the Enter key to
open it).

Icon types

When you use Windows, you'll run across lots of different types
of icons. In the Program Manager, the icons you'll most frequently
bump into are the following:

Icon Name	*What It Means*
Program-item	Represents an application (program) that you can start in Windows.
	Program-item icons are located in group windows (see "Creating a Group" in Part III, "Program Manager"). You can move a program to a new group window by dragging its program-item icon to the group window.
Application	Represents an application (program) that's running in Windows but whose window is currently minimized (referred to as "reducing an application window to an icon").
	Application icons are usually located along the bottom of the Windows desktop.
Group	Represents a group window that's been minimized (see "Sizing a Window" later in Part I).

10 Icons

In the File Manager, the icons you most frequently encounter are the following:

Icon Name	What It Means
Drive	Represents the different disk drives on your system.
	These icons are located at the top of the File Manager window (see "Parts of a Directory Window" in Part IV, "File Manager").
Directory	Represents the various directories on the selected drive.
	Directories are listed by name in alphabetical order on the left side of the Directory Window (see "Parts of a Directory Window" in Part IV, "File Manager").
Current directory	Represents the drive that is currently selected.
	The files in this directory appear on the right side of the Directory Window (see "Parts of a Directory Window" in Part IV, "File Manager").
Program file	Represents a program or batch file that starts the particular application.
	Common filename extensions for program file icons are EXE, COM, BAT, and PIF.
Document file	Represents a file that is associated with a particular application like Word for Windows or Excel.
	When you open a document file icon in the File Manager, Windows automatically starts the associated application.
System file	Represents a system file or hidden file (see "Changing File Attributes" in Part IV, "File Manager" for details).
File	Represents a standard file that is not associated with an application, nor is it marked with a system or hidden attribute.

See the example in *Windows 3.1 For Dummies*, 2nd Edition, Chapter 4, "Icons."

More stuff

In some circumstances, you can perform tasks with icons by using the *drag and drop* method, derived from dragging a window from one place and dropping it in another.

Moving a Window

Used to get at a window that may be covered up by another window or to move a window out of the way for the time being.

To move a window, click and hold the left mouse button on the window's title bar and then move the window in the direction you want it to go. When you arrive at your intended destination for the window, just release the mouse button.

Steps

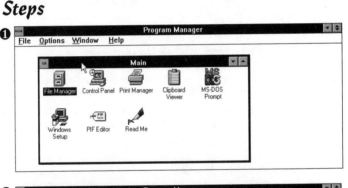

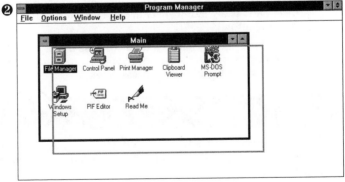

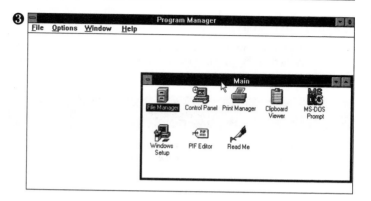

❸

See the example in *Windows 3.1 For Dummies*, 2nd Edition, Chapter 7, "Arranging Things (Moving Windows Around)."

More stuff

By clicking a window's title bar (see "Parts of a Window" later in Part I if you don't know a title bar from a title page), you make that window active — bringing the window to the top of a pile in some cases — and make the window ready to be moved.

Moving a window from one place to another is also known as *drag and drop*. This term is derived from dragging the window from one place and dropping it in another.

Keep in mind that a maximized window cannot be moved unless it's restored by pressing the *restore button*, which is the funny two-headed arrow in the top right corner of a window's title bar. (See "Parts of a Window" later in Part I for information on the restore button.)

If you don't have a mouse, you can also use the keyboard to move a window. Press Alt, the spacebar, and M. After moving the window with the arrow keys, press Enter.

Parts of a Window

Components used in Windows and Windows programs to change dimensions of a window and to accomplish different actions within that window.

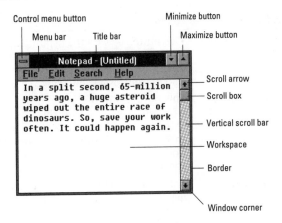

Control menu button
Menu bar
Title bar
Minimize button
Maximize button

Notepad - [Untitled]

File Edit Search Help

In a split second, 65-million
years ago, a huge asteroid
wiped out the entire race of
dinosaurs. So, save your work
often. It could happen again.

Scroll arrow
Scroll box
Vertical scroll bar
Workspace
Border
Window corner

—— Restore button

Window Part	Function
Border	The thin line that separates a lonely window from the outside world.
	A window's border can be used to change the size of the window. If a window doesn't have a border, it can't be sized.
Control menu button	This button offers a pull-down menu with a variety of selections for manipulating the size of a window, closing a window, and switching to other windows (see "Control Menu" earlier in Part I for information on this button).
	Double-clicking the control menu button closes a window.
Menu bar	The pull-down menus from this bar allow you to get at all available commands a window has to offer while keeping the window clean and tidy when not in use. Just click a word in the menu bar, and a list of options comes spilling out.
	Most menu bars have file, edit, and help menus. Another way of doing the same thing is by pressing the Alt key and the underlined letter of a word on the menu bar. To exit the menu bar, just press the Esc key. Sorry, no appetizers on this menu.

(continues)

Window Part	Function
Maximize button	This button — with the aspiring up arrow in it — causes a window to fill up the entire screen. Pressing Alt, the spacebar, and X also maximizes a window.
Minimize button	This button — with the sad down arrow in it — causes a window to shrink to a little icon at the bottom of the screen (see "Icons" earlier in Part I if you don't know an icon from an ice cube). Pressing Alt, the spacebar, and N also minimizes a window.
Restore button	This funny two-headed button restores — hence the name — a maximized or mini-mized window back to a reasonable size. Pressing Alt, the spacebar, and R also restores a window.
Scroll arrow	Two of these arrows appear on what's called a vertical scroll bar. The up arrow on this bar pulls the scroll box up and pushes whatever is inside the workspace down toward the bottom of the screen.
	The down arrow pushes the scroll box down and pulls whatever is inside the workspace up toward the top of the screen.
Scroll box	This little box shows you whether you're at the top, middle, or bottom of your workspace by its position on the vertical scroll bar.
	You can move up and down in a window by clicking and dragging the scroll box in either direction. The PgUp and PgDn keys move the scroll box as well as what's in the window.
Title bar	The title bar resides at the top of a window and serves as a handle for the window. The title bar lists the name of the application the window represents and any open file within the window.
	If you are working within a window, the title bar of the window is a different color than any other open window. This different color indicates that the window is active, which allows you to tell which window you are currently working in. By double-clicking the title bar, you maximize the window.

Pull-Down Menus 15

Window Part	Function
Vertical scroll bar	This bar — on the right side of the window — houses the vertical scroll box and two scrolling arrows.
	You can easily move within a window by clicking within the vertical scroll bar. To view toward the top or bottom of a window, just click the corresponding place in the scroll bar. Some windows have a scroll bar at the bottom and allow you to view side to side as opposed to up and down.
Window corner	Moving to the lower right window corner changes the mouse pointer to an arrow with two heads.
	This diagonal two-headed arrow allows you to resize the window both vertically and horizontally at the same time. Click and hold the left mouse button with this arrow and change the window's dimensions.
Workspace	This area is usually the blank space inside of the window, just waiting to be filled by your creative juices.

See the example in *Windows 3.1 For Dummies*, 2nd Edition, Chapter 6, "Examining All Those Buttons, Bars, and Boxes."

Pull-Down Menus

Allows you to work within a window by selecting menus and choosing commands.

Pull-down menus let you get at all available commands a window has to offer while keeping the workspace in the window clean and tidy when not in use. The pull-down menu contains a number of commands such as File, Edit, and Help. To display a pull-down menu, you simply click with the left mouse button on one of the options on the horizontal menu bar. After making a new selection in a pull-down menu, press the left mouse button or the Enter key to put it into effect. To close a pull-down menu without making a selection, press the Esc key twice, choose another pull-down, or click in the workspace.

Steps

❶

Notepad - LAWN.TXT

File Edit Search Help

Don't forget to water the plants on Tuesday or they might just dry up.
Jeez, if I only had an automatic sprinkler system.

❷

Notepad - LAWN.TXT

File Edit Search Help

New
Open...
Save
Save As...
Print
Page Setup...
Print Setup...
Exit

o water the plants on Tuesday or they might just dry
y had an automatic sprinkler system.

Common Options	What They Do
File	This pull-down menu contains file-related options, such as New, Open, Save, and Print.
Edit	This pull-down menu allows editing functions to the text or images inside the window, such as Cut, Copy, or Paste.
Help	This often-present pull-down menu lets you get help on what's going on inside the window (see "Windows Help" later in Part I for more information on this command).

See the example in *Windows 3.1 For Dummies*, 2nd Edition, Chapter 5, "Finding the Secret Pull-Down Menus."

More stuff

You can alternatively select a command in a pull-down menu by pressing the Alt key and using the left- or right-arrow keys to highlight the different commands on the menu bar. Pressing the Enter key, once you have the word you want highlighted, displays the commands on the pull-down menu. For example, you can press the Alt key and move to the Edit command by pressing on the right arrow once.

After you have the Edit command highlighted, you can press Enter to display all the commands that are stored under Edit. You can then use the up- or down- arrow keys to move to different commands on the menu. Press Enter to select the command or press Esc twice to exit back to the workspace.

Another way to select a command is to use the Alt-Underlined letter combination. For example, by pressing on the Alt key and the H key simultaneously, you can activate the Help pull-down menu. Notice that each letter in the menu bar is underlined. You can continue to hold down the Alt key and then press the underlined key for the command you want to choose. Alternatively, you can use the up- and down- arrow keys to select the command and press Enter to have that command carried out or press the Esc key a few times to exit back to the workspace.

Some commands in a pull-down menu have shortcut keys; you can see them to the right of a command. Using a shortcut key combination is one of the fastest ways to execute a command, bypassing clicking with the mouse, the arrow keys, and the Alt key combinations altogether.

Some commands have a check mark or a bullet to the left of the command itself. This indicator lets you know that the command is active, and it is usually used when there are several sub-commands within a command. For example, subcommands like Outline, Normal, and Page Layout are different views within a View command in a word processor.

Some command names are followed by an ellipsis (...). Choosing this kind of command displays a dialog box (see "Dialog Boxes" earlier in Part I for explanations of these types of boxes). If the command is followed by two greater-than symbols (>>), choosing the button expands the current pull-down menu to display more choices. If the command name is dimmed, the command is temporarily off-limits.

Sizing a Window

Used when moving a window just doesn't do the trick.

Sizing a window allows you to have several windows displayed simultaneously without making the screen seem too crowded. To size the window both vertically and horizontally, move to the lower right window corner. Moving to this position changes the mouse arrow to a diagonal two-headed arrow. This arrow allows you to resize the window both vertically and horizontally at the same time. Click and hold the left mouse button with this arrow and change the windows dimensions.

Steps

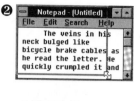

See the example in *Windows 3.1 For Dummies*, 2nd Edition, Chapter 7, "Arranging Things (Moving Windows Around)."

More stuff

You can just change a window's width by positioning the mouse arrow on either the left or right vertical border of the window. The mouse arrow changes from an arrow with one head to one with two heads. Click and hold the left mouse button while you move the mouse either right or left. Let go of the mouse button when the window is the right size.

You can also change just a window's height by positioning the mouse arrow on either the top or bottom horizontal border of the window. The arrow changes from an arrow with one head to one with two heads. Click and hold the left mouse button while you move the mouse either up or down. Release the mouse button when the window is the right size.

If you don't have a mouse or don't want to use it, you can also use the keyboard to size a window. Press Alt, the spacebar, and S (this option is grayed out if the window is maximized). This keyboard combination begins the sizing process. The mouse arrow changes to a cross, and the outline of the window changes colors. Once you start the sizing process with one of the arrow keys, the cross changes back to an arrow. Using the left- or right-arrow keys sizes the window horizontally; using the up- or down-arrow key sizes the window vertically. Press Enter when you finish sizing the window. If you change your mind and want the window back to its original size while sizing the window, press Esc.

You can use the maximize button — in the upper right-hand corner, with the aspiring up arrow in it — to have a window fill up the entire screen. Pressing Alt, the spacebar, and X will also maximize a window.

You can use the minimize button — in the upper right corner, with the sad down arrow in it — to cause a window to shrink to a little icon at the bottom of the screen (see "Icons" earlier in Part I if you don't know an icon from an ice tray). When you minimize a window, it just sits at the bottom of the screen — usually with a name underneath it — waiting for you to double-click it with the mouse so it can come back to its former size. Pressing Alt, the spacebar, and N also minimizes a window.

If a window is either maximized or minimized, the funny two-headed button in the upper right-hand corner restores (hence the name) the maximized or minimized window back to a reasonable size. Pressing Alt, the spacebar, and R will also restore a window.

Starting Windows

The WIN command is used to start Microsoft Windows from the DOS prompt. To start windows, type **WIN** at the **C:\>** prompt and press the Enter key.

Steps

❶ `c:\>`

❷ `c:\>Win`

See the example in *Windows 3.1 For Dummies*, 2nd Edition, Chapter 1, "What Is Windows?"

More stuff

Sometimes DOS can't find Windows. If you get a DOS cryptic error message like `Bad command or file name`, it's time for you to do a little DOS magic. Try typing **cd\windows** and pressing the Enter key. Now, retype **WIN** and press the Enter key one more time. This usually jump-starts Windows and doesn't drain your battery (see "Windows Modes" later in Part I for an explanation of the different ways Windows can start up).

You can impress you friends with your Windows knowledge by typing **WIN**, a space, and then a colon (:). This little command just prevents showing the opening screen while Windows is starting. It's kinda like fast forwarding through the movie credits with your VCR.

Types of Windows

The two basic types of windows are application (program) windows and document windows. Program windows are those being used by an application that is currently running. Document windows are smaller windows within a program window that hold text or graphics that you can work on.

Program window

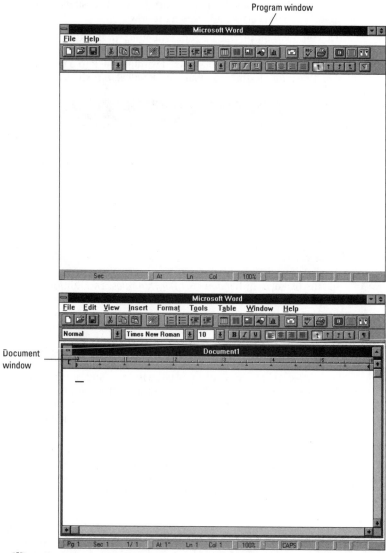

Document window

See the example in *Windows 3.1 For Dummies*, 2nd Edition, Chapter 7, "Arranging Things (Moving Windows Around)."

More stuff

Document windows don't have their own menu bars, nor do they
have wet bars. They do, however, have their own title bars unless
they are maximized (see "Parts of a Window" earlier in Part I if
you can't tell the difference between maximized and your neighbor,
Maxine), in which case they share the application's title bar.

You can usually have more than one document window open in
an application window at any one time.

Windows Help

Windows has its own help system, which can answer questions
about commands or features. You can get to the help system by
pressing the F1 key on your keyboard.

Steps

❶

❷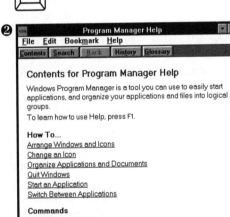

Help	Option
Contents	Clicking on this main command with your left mouse button displays the help options. Choose Table of Contents to display all the topics for the active program. Another command button — called Instructions — within this window gives you directions on how to get through the help system.
Search	This command button brings up a search dialog box where you can type in a word and have the help system show you related topics. Following the Iinstructions on this dialog box can make your life easier.
Back	This command button will let you backtrack through the help system that you have trotted through. This option will be grayed out if you haven't gone anywhere in the help system yet.
History	Similar to the Back command button, it shows you a list of the help topics that you viewed during that session. You can click with your left mouse button on anywhere that you have been to instantly go back there.
Glossary	This command button gives you an alphabetical listing of terms used in the Windows on-line help system.

See the example in *Windows 3.1 For Dummies*, 2nd Edition, Chapter 19, "Help on the Windows Help System."

More stuff

You can exit the help window by double-clicking the control menu button in the upper left-hand corner of the help window (see "Control Menu" earlier in Part I for information on this box).

Several commands on the Help pull-down menu (see "Parts of a Window" earlier in Part I for an explanation of the menu bar and pull-down menus) vary from program to program. Of these commands, there is usually one that says Contents or Index, which can be accessed faster by simply pressing the F1 key.

One advantage to left mouse-clicking the Help pull-down, however, is that the very last option on the bottom is usually an "About" command that gives information about the current program and what mode your system is running in (see "Windows Modes" later in Part I for an explanation of modes). It can be very important on those technical support calls to product vendors. It's also a fun thing to look at when you're trying to avoid work.

Each program that comes with Windows or that you can buy for
Windows has a help system designed just for it. If you go out and
buy *Earl's Windmill Maker for Windows,* it will usually have a help
menu that will at the very least tell who wrote the program. Some
programs for Windows have a help system that surpasses the
documentation that comes with them!

Windows Modes

Windows 3.1 can start up in two operating modes when you type
WIN: *Standard* mode and *386 Enhanced* mode. Windows selects
which is the best one for your machine. If you have a 286 computer, you will start up in Standard mode. If you have a 386 or 486
computer with two megabytes of extended memory, your
computer will start up in 386 Enhanced mode.

Mode	Description
Standard Mode **(WIN /S)**	Standard mode has two advantages: Standard mode can run faster, and Stan- dard mode allows 286 machines — which can't run Enhanced mode — to run Windows.
386 Enhanced Mode **(WIN or WIN/3)**	The 386 Enhanced mode (also known as just Enhanced mode) takes advantage of the horsepower of the 386 or 486 micro- processor. Two of the main advantages to Enhanced mode are the ability to run DOS applications in a window and using hard disk space like it was memory (referred to as virtual memory), allowing you to have more applications running at the same time.

See the example in *Windows 3.1 For Dummies*, 2nd Edition,
Chapter 15, "Memory Stuff You'll Want to Forget." Also see the
example in *Windows 3.1 For Dummies*, 2nd Edition, Chapter 18,
"Error Messages (What You Did Does Not Compute)," and the
example in *MORE Windows For Dummies*, Chapter 17, "Running
Out of Memory."

More stuff

With Windows 3.0, there was one other mode called *Real* mode
that doesn't exist in Windows 3.1. Real mode allowed machines
like PCs and XTs and machines with very little memory to run
Windows. This mode was removed in Windows 3.1 mainly
because Windows on an XT is too slow, and, on a PC or XT,
Windows couldn't show off its cool screen colors.

Sometimes you may run a program that was designed for a version of Windows previous to Windows 3.0. You'll know if this is the case because you'll get a HUGE box on the screen that has at the very top `Application Compatibility Warning` written in some alerting color. If you find yourself in this situation, it's probably time that you go out looking for a newer version of the program that will work with Windows 3.0 and above. If you decide to continue — and I recommend against it — Windows may suddenly hiccup and kick you out to the DOS prompt without warning.

Part II:
Application Basics

Arranging Application Windows

Allows a user to have all running applications arranged and visible on the Windows desktop.

With the left mouse button, double-click anywhere there is open space on the desktop. A Task List box appears. Using the left mouse button, click on the Tile command button. Press the Esc key to exit from the Task List box without rearranging your desktop.

Steps

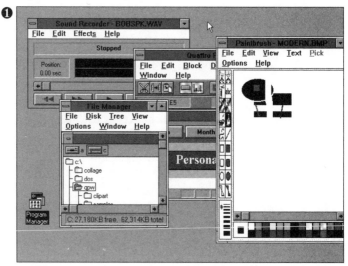

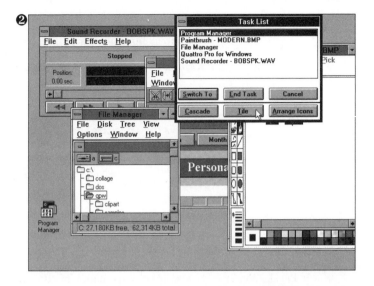

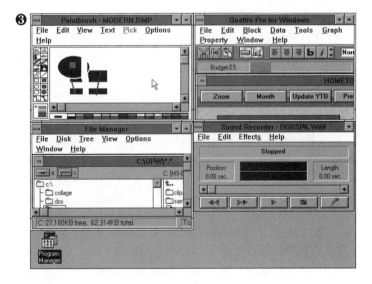

Of the many command buttons on the Task List box, which keeps track of all the open programs and lets you switch between them, these two command buttons are the cool ones:

Button	*What It Does*
Tile	Arranges applications by making them small enough to fit neatly in a tile pattern. The more windows you have open, the more tiles you have.
	Pressing Ctrl+Esc, Alt+T also starts the Tile command.
Cascade	Arranges applications by making all of the application windows the same size and then overlapping them so only the title bar of each window shows. The cascade arrangement makes the open application windows look like you've just neatly spread out a deck of cards.
	Pressing Ctrl+Esc, Alt+C also starts the tile command. Clicking on a card brings it to the top of the deck.

See "Dialog Boxes" in Part I, "Windows Basics," if you don't know a command button from a cotton snake. See "Parts of a Window" in Part I, "Windows Basics," for an explanation of title bars.

More stuff

The Tile and Cascade command buttons only deal with arranging open windows. If you've got icons spread across the bottom of your screen and open windows all over the place, you can arrange all of these applications another way. Since a person really only deals with one application at a time (popular research tells us), maximizing one window is probably the better (not to mention the easier) solution.

See "Icons" in Part I, "Windows Basics," for an explanation of these little buggers.

Having only one window open doesn't mean that the applications that have been turned into icons aren't working; it just means that those applications are not cluttering up your screen and wasting memory.

First, you must minimize all of your application windows by clicking on the minimize button (the downward-pointing arrow in the upper right-hand corner of each window). Then you double-click on the icon that represents the application that you want to use (a good one is Solitaire).

Now, there are two routes you can take here, but they both lead to the same destination: the Task List box. You can either double-click on the desktop, or you can use the Ctrl+Esc keyboard combination to get to the Task List box. When the Task List box is open, click on the Tile command button to arrange your desktop in a way-cool fashion.

If you happen to have all of your applications turned into icons
and they just won't line up or are a housekeeping nightmare,
there is one other thing you can do. First, using your left mouse
button, double-click on the desktop. When the Task List box
appears, click on the Arrange Icons command button. Presto! All
of your icons are neatly arranged along the bottom of your
desktop.

Changing the Size of the Font in a Non-Windows Application

You can change the size of fonts displayed in the window when
you're running a non-Windows application (like WordPerfect 5.1
or Lotus 1-2-3 for DOS) in a window in 386 Enhanced mode.

Click on the application window's control menu button (the box
in the upper left corner with the small bar in its middle). Select
Fonts, and a Font Selection dialog box appears. After making new
selections in the dialog box, press the Enter key to put them into
effect. To exit the Font Selection box without making changes,
press the Esc key.

Steps

❶

```
                              LIST
LIST File Selection      1 of 14      Path C:\*.*
COLLAGE
DOS
QPW
VAULT
WINDOWS
WINMAST
WINWORD
AUTOEXEC.BAT
COMMAND .COM
CONFIG  .SYS
IO      .SYS
LIST    .COM
MSDOS   .SYS
WINA20  .386

Files: 14     ♦ Used: 152692    ♦ Free: 26781696  ♦ F3=Menu  F1=Help  F10=Exit
```

File Manager   Paintbrush -   Sound   Quattro Pro for   Program   MS-DOS
                 MODERN.BMP   Recorder -   Windows   Manager   Prompt
                               BDBSPK.WAV

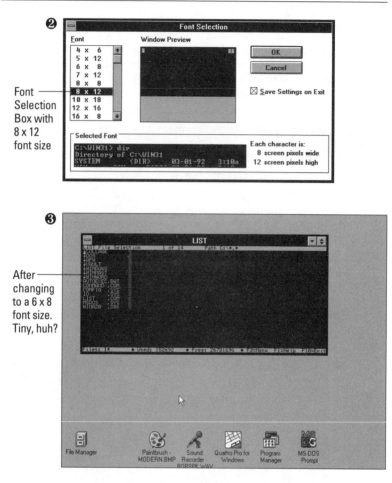

Font Selection Box with 8 x 12 font size

After changing to a 6 x 8 font size. Tiny, huh?

More stuff

If you want to change the size of the font in a non-Windows window, but all you seem to get is a full-screen session of your non-Windows application (even after you press Alt+Enter, which is a neat way to toggle between window and full-screen), you may not be in 386 Enhanced mode even if you are running on a 386 or 486 computer. You can only run a non-Windows application in a window if you are running in 386 Enhanced mode.

See "Windows Modes" in Part I, "Windows Basics," for an explanation of modes.

In the Font list box, a variety of sizes from 4 x 6 to 16 x 8 are shown. These numbers represent the size of the font in what is called *pixels* — just a fancy word meaning a lot of little dots. Smaller font size numbers make for smaller words and a smaller window. Bigger fonts are good if you don't always have your reading glasses handy. The Window Preview box shows the size of the window in relation to the desktop.

The Save Settings on Exit check box is an important one. If you click on this box, you save the changes that you made in terms of window size and font for this window. Doing this is a good idea if you like the window size, especially since you can't change the size of the window for a non-Windows application with the mouse.

See "Dialog Boxes" in Part I, "Windows Basics," for an explanation of check boxes.

Changing the size of the font also changes the size of the window, but some of the combinations aren't always the most pleasing to the eye.

DOS programs that display mostly text (like Lotus 1-2-3 or WordStar) work well in non-Windows application windows. Graphics programs, however, occasionally have problems in a non-Windows application window; sometimes they don't fit in the window or their colors aren't right.

It's time to switch from a window to full-screen by pressing the Alt+Enter keyboard combination. There, isn't that better?

You can also take a look at the Video Mode selection in the PIF editor to see whether there is any difference between what's displayed in Text mode and what's displayed in a higher video mode. If you really want to see the program in a window, you can see whether the vendor of your application makes a Windows version, or you can shell out the bucks and buy a higher resolution graphics card, which gives you even more graphics modes to support the non-Windows application in a window.

See "PIF Editor" in Part III, "Program Manager," for the lowdown on PIFs.

If you want to move information from a non-Windows application to another application, see "Transferring Information between Applications."

Changing the Settings for Running a Non-Windows Application

When running a non-Windows application (like Word 5.5 or Lotus Agenda for DOS) in a window in 386 Enhanced mode, you can change the display, tasking, and priority, and you can terminate the non-Windows application.

Select the control menu by clicking the window's control menu button, the box in the upper left-corner with the small bar in its middle. Select Settings, and a dialog box appears. Make new selections in the dialog box, and press the Enter key to put them into effect. To exit the dialog box without making changes, press the Esc key.

Steps

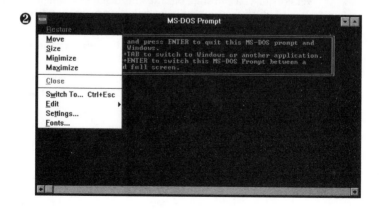

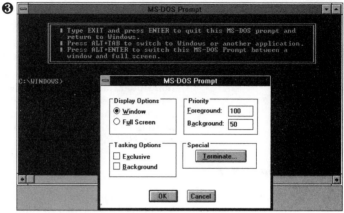

Display Option Name	What It Does
Window	Changes the current non-Windows application to a window if it isn't already a window.
Full screen	Changes the current non-Windows application to a full-screen session if it isn't already full-screen.

Tasking Option Name	What It Does
Exclusive	Stops other applications from doing anything but allows this application to continue running. This is a DOS hogging option.
Background	Runs the non-Windows application in the background while letting you work on other Windows applications, unless one of the other Windows applications has Exclusive on and is doing work.

Priority Option Name	What It Does
Foreground	Tells how fast the non-Windows application runs in relation to other Windows applications when it is the active application.
Background	Tells how fast the non-Windows application would run in relation to other non-Windows applications when it isn't the active application. This setting only matters if Background has been set in the Tasking Options box.

More stuff

You can only run a non-Windows application in a window when Windows is running in 386 Enhanced mode. (See "Windows Modes" in Part I, "Windows Basics," to find out what mode you're in.)

If, every time you bring up a non-Windows application, it comes up in a full-screen session instead of a window, see "PIF Editor" in Part III, "Program Manager," to get the scoop on starting up in a window for those non-Windows applications.

Sometimes a non-Windows application freaks out when it runs in a window. That's where the Terminate button comes into play. If you find that you are stuck with a misbehaving non-Windows application, try pressing the Esc key a couple of times. If this doesn't work, press the Alt+Enter key combination to change from a window to a full-screen session. If that doesn't fix the problem, change back to a window by pressing Alt+Enter again and open the control menu (click the control menu button or press Alt+spacebar) and select Settings.

The Terminate button in the Special box is really the button of last resort. Pressing this button causes you to lose all data in the window that you may have been working on. If you are stuck in a full-screen DOS session, you can also press Ctrl+Alt+Del to quit the application. You get a message asking whether you are sure of this drastic measure. Choose Yes. Again, use the Terminate button or the Ctrl+Alt+Del key combination only as a last resort.

Quitting an Application

Do this when you're finished working in an active application.

Press the Alt+F4 key combination. Before exiting, Windows asks whether you want to save anything that you haven't saved already. Press Enter to save and exit; press Esc to return to the application.

Steps

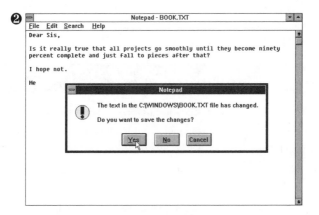

❶
```
Notepad - BOOK.TXT
File  Edit  Search  Help
Dear Sis,

Is it really true that all projects go smoothly until they become ninety
percent complete and just fall to pieces after that?

I hope not.

Me|
```

❷
```
Notepad - BOOK.TXT
File  Edit  Search  Help
Dear Sis,

Is it really true that all projects go smoothly until they become ninety
percent complete and just fall to pieces after that?

I hope not.

Me
              Notepad
   ⚠  The text in the C:\WINDOWS\BOOK.TXT file has changed.
      Do you want to save the changes?
              Yes    No    Cancel
```

See the example in *Windows 3.1 For Dummies,* 2nd Edition, Chapter 4, "Windows Stuff Everybody Thinks You Already Know."

More stuff

If you're running a non-Windows application and you want to exit, exiting the application usually closes the window or the full-screen session. If this doesn't happen, try typing the word **EXIT** at the DOS prompt.

Double-clicking on the application's control button or pressing Alt+F4 also exits an application.

See "Control Menu" in Part I, "Windows Basics," for another way to shut down your application.

If you're trying to exit Windows — by double-clicking on the Program Manager's Control button — and you get a pesky error message telling you `Application still active`, you left a non-Windows application running.

Press Ctrl+Esc to bring up the Task List box and see what non-Windows application is hidden in the background. Double-click on the name of the culprit to switch to it and then close the application.

Never, but *never*, quit an application or Windows by just turning off your computer's power switch. In Windows etiquette, turning the system off without properly closing it down is akin to leaving a restaurant without paying the bill. It's not a pleasant sight. Just exit all of your applications and then exit Windows before you turn off your computer's power. Everyone will be happier in the long run.

Always save your work before you exit a program or Windows and turn your computer off.

Starting an Application

You must start an application before you can run it.

Inside the Program Manager, double-click on the Games group icon. Select the Solitaire application by double-clicking on the Solitaire icon.

Steps

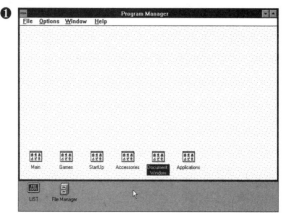

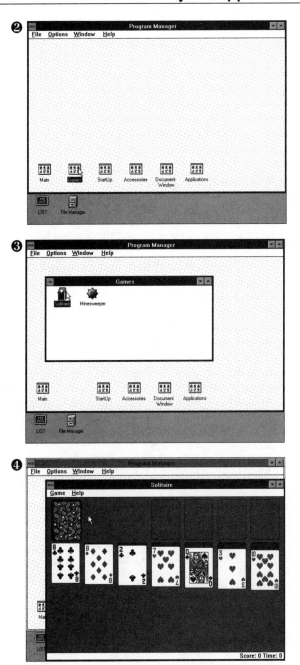

See the example in *Windows 3.1 For Dummies,* 2nd Edition, Chapter 5, "Starting your favorite program," and the example in *MORE Windows For Dummies*, Chapter 20, "How Can I Bypass My Startup Group?"

More stuff

There are several ways to open an application:

- Double-click on the icon that represents the application you want to run.

- Double-click on a filename in the File Manager or a program information file in the File Manager.

See "Starting an Application in the File Manager" in Part IV, "File Manager."

- Use the DOS command prompt to open non-Windows applications.

- Use the keyboard. Hold down the Ctrl key and press the Tab key until the window holding the icon representing the application that you want is highlighted. Use the arrow keys to select the application. Press Enter.

  If the icon is hiding within a program group, press Ctrl+Tab until the program group you want is selected, and press Enter.

See "Opening a Group Window" in Part III, "Program Manager," for information on these funky icons.

- Select File, Run on the Program Manager menu bar. After the Run dialog box opens, start typing the program's filename. Better yet, click on the Browse key to look for the file.

After you've started a couple of applications and wandered from window to window, you may want to start Solitaire — or any application — again. Stop for a minute. Did you close it the last time you used it? Is the application sitting there at the bottom of the screen as an icon just waiting for you to use it again? If you're not sure, use the Task List box (press Ctrl+Esc) to check before you open a new copy of the same application. Opening the same application multiple times, especially if you're entering data in multiple copies of the application at the same time, causes lots of headaches and wastes memory.

See "Icons" in Part I, "Windows Basics," if you want to know the difference between an icon and an ICBM.

Starting a Non-Windows Application

You can start a non-Windows application or a DOS program by starting a DOS session or opening a DOS window and typing in the filname of the application.

Steps

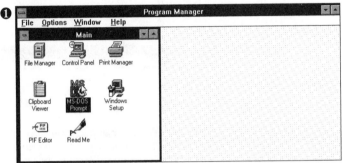

More stuff

Another way to start a non-Windows application is to select File, Run on the Program Manager's menu bar. After the Run dialog box opens, start typing the program's filename. Better yet, play with the Browse key to look for the file.

Also see "PIF Editor" in Part III, "Program Manager," for more information on starting non-Windows applications.

Switching between Applications

Lets you get from one application to another in Windows.

Hold down the Alt key and press Tab. A small box with an application name in it appears every time you press Tab. Release the keys to go to the program highlighted in the box.

Steps

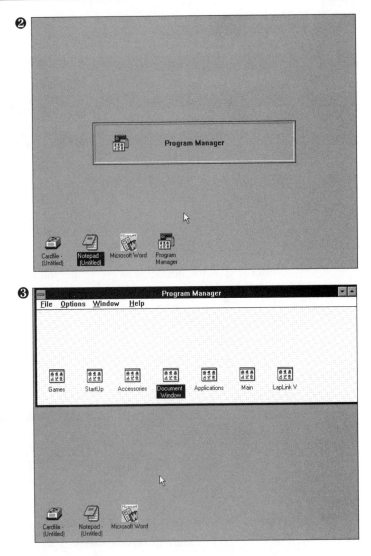

More stuff

Sometimes the Alt+Tab combination doesn't work in the cool fashion you should get accustomed to. If this is the case, open the Control Panel and click on the Fast 'Alt+Tab' Switching check box.

See "Changing Desktop Options" in Part V, "Control Panel," for information on this little known hot spot.

Another — but not so fun — way to switch between applications is to double-click anywhere there is open space on the desktop. The Task List box appears. Select the name of the application and click on the Switch To command button, or just double-click on the application's name.

Transferring Information between Applications

Used when you move information between applications. Achieved by using the Cut, Copy, and Paste commands.

1. Place the mouse pointer at the start of the information you want to copy.

2. Click and hold down the mouse button and drag the mouse until you select all of the information that you want to copy. (Selected information changes color.)

3. Release the mouse button when everything you want to move is highlighted.

4. Click on Edit from the menu bar and select Copy.

5. Click the place in the document window where you want to copy the information.

6. Choose Edit from the menu bar and select Paste.

Steps

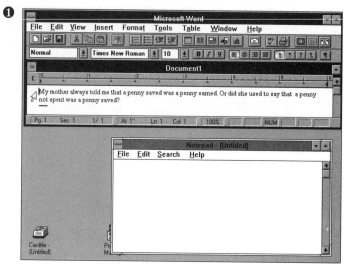

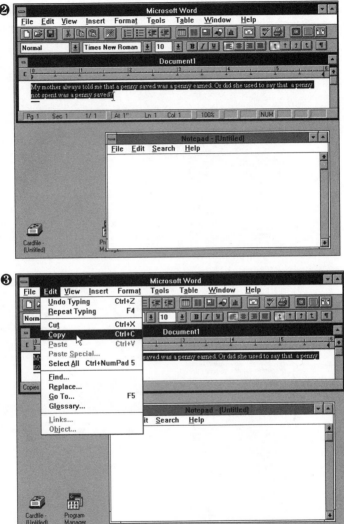

❹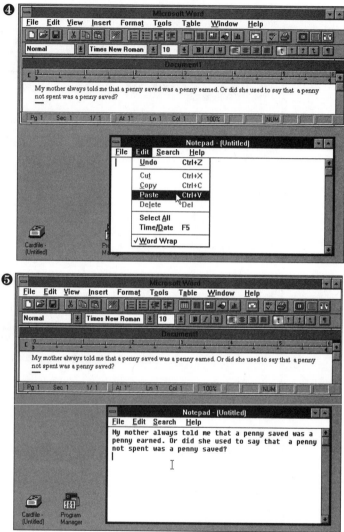

❺

See the examples in *Windows 3.1 For Dummies,* 2nd Edition, Chapter 9, "Sharing Information (Moving Words, Pictures, and Sounds Around)."

More stuff

On the menu bar in most windows applications is an Edit pull-down menu. This menu usually has commands like Cut, Copy, and Paste. The Cut and Copy commands are similar in that they move information from one place to a holding area called the *Clipboard*. (See "Clipboard" in Part III, "Program Manager.")

The difference between Cut and Copy is that Cut deletes the selection from the first application and moves it to the Clipboard. Copy duplicates the information to the Clipboard and leaves it in the first application.

The Paste command is grayed unless there is some information in the Clipboard. Select the place in the application that you want to paste the information and then choose Paste from the Edit pull-down menu.

Here are the keyboard shortcuts: Cut is Ctrl+X, Copy is Ctrl+C, and Paste is Ctrl+V.

Sometimes — if you're lucky — the application that you are working in has icon buttons that represent these frequently used options. Find out! Cut, Copy, and Paste icons can be lifesavers, not to mention that they save your fingers from pressing all those keyboard combinations.

Sometimes in the Edit pull-down menu is a Select All option. This option selects all the information in the current document window and waits for you to copy it to the Clipboard.

To move information from non-Windows to a Windows application, follow these steps:

1. When using a non-Windows application in a window, click on the Control button. Click on Edit, Mark (which is the way you start to select information in a DOS window).

2. Click and hold down the mouse button with the mouse pointer at the beginning of the text that you want to copy.

3. While still pressing the mouse button, drag the mouse to the end of the text selection and then let go of the mouse button.

4. Click on the control button. Click on Edit, Copy to move the information to the Clipboard. Alternatively, pressing Enter also copies the selection to the Clipboard.

5. Open the application that you want to paste information into and select Edit, Paste from the menu bar.

See "Pull-Down Menus" in Part I, "Windows Basics."

After you highlight a selection to cut or copy, select Cut or Copy from the Edit menu right away; otherwise, you could inadvertently click the mouse button or press a key somewhere else in the document and accidentally unselect the highlighted information.

Part III:
Program Manager

Arranging Group Icons

Used when the icons in the Program Manager are no longer visible, no longer lie on top of each other, or are in no discernible order.

To rearrange group icons, select the Main group icon in the Program Manager; then from the Windows menu bar, click on Window, Arrange Icons to evenly distribute the group icons along the lower left edge of the Program Manager window.

Steps

❶

❷
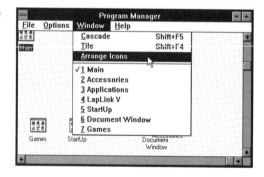

❸
```
━                    Program Manager              ▾ ▲
  File   Options   Window   Help

              ⟍

  ▦▦▦       ▦▦▦
  Applications   Main

  ▦▦▦     ▦▦▦     ▦▦▦     ▦▦▦     ▦▦▦
  LapLink V   Games   StartUp   Document   Accessories
                              Window
```

More stuff

The real difference between group icons and program icons is
that the group icons act like folders and hold application icons
inside of them. That's why when you double-click on a group
icon, you see program icons inside. You can also cascade and tile
program group windows within the Program Manager.

 See "Arranging Application Windows" in Part II, "Application
Basics," if you think that Cascade and Tile have something to do
with dishwashers and kitchen floors.

Using the mouse, you can drag the individual group icons to a
new location, or you can use the keyboard:

1. Press Alt+- (hyphen) to open the group icon's control
   menu, or click on the Control button once.

See "Control Button" in Part I, "Windows Basics," for information
about the control button.

2. Click on the Move command.

3. Use the arrow keys to get the group icon to the place in the
   Program Manager that you want.

4. Press Enter to anchor the icon, or press Esc to abort the
   move operation.

You can have Windows automatically rearrange application icons
in a window. (This is really cool, and I use it all the time, but that
may be because I'm a neat freak.) Once this option is on, it's like
having a rubber band on the icons. If you pull the icon out of its
neat little pattern, it goes bouncing right back to its nice forma-
tion.

1. From the Program Manager menu bar, click on Options.

2. Select Auto Arrange (a check mark beside the command means it's in effect).

When Auto Arrange has a check mark next to it, Windows automatically rearranges application icons whenever you change the size of a window, add new icons to a window, or move icons from one window to another. Unfortunately, Auto Arrange only works with application icons and doesn't work with group icons.

You can arrange application icons within the Program Manager the same way you arrange group icons:

1. Click on the group window that contains the application icons you want to rearrange.

2. On the menu bar, click on Window.

3. Click on Arrange Icons to distribute the application icons evenly within the selected group window.

Most application icons are usually unique to the application, but the same can't be said with group icons. Group icons all look the same when they're lined up at the bottom of the Program Manager window. The only difference between group icons is the name underneath each icon.

To make a group icon change to a window, double-click on the icon. Later, if you try to close a group in the Program Manager's window by double-clicking the control button, which normally closes an application, the window doesn't close; it just turns into a group icon at the bottom of the Program Manager. You can permanently get rid of a group window or group icon; see "Deleting a Group" later in this section for instructions.

Some group windows have so many icons packed inside them that you may not be able to see all the application icons. If some icons are outside the edge of a window, the window has scroll bars along the right and bottom edge. Click on a scroll bar, and the icons move into view.

See "Parts of a Window" in Part I, "Windows Basics," if you don't know the difference between a scroll bar and a wet bar.

Changing Program Manager Options

Used primarily to change default options of the Program Manager.

Steps

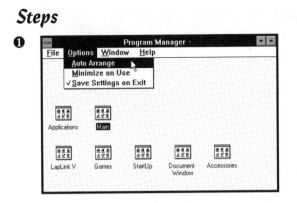

What It's Called	What It Does
Auto Arrange	Rearranges the application icons in a group window whenever you add application icons, change the size of a window, or move application icons. A check mark next to the command means that it's on.
	Here's the keyboard shortcut: from the Program Manager, press Alt, O, A.
Minimize on Use	Shrinks the Program Manager window to an icon whenever you start an application, unless the application you want to run starts as an icon. The Program Manager icon resides on the bottom of the desktop. A check mark next to the command means it's on.
	Here's the keyboard shortcut: from the Program Manager, press Alt, O, M.
Save Settings on Exit	Lets you save the order of the windows and icons in Program Manager when you exit Windows. A check mark next to the command means it's on.
	Here's the keyboard shortcut: from the Program Manager, press Alt, O, S.

Clipboard

Used as a holding tank for information when the Cut or Copy commands are used in an application.

To see what's in the Clipboard after a Cut or Copy command, open the Program Manager, double-click on the Main group icon to open the Main window, and double-click on the Clipboard Viewer application icon. Inside the Clipboard is the information that you cut or copied.

Steps

❶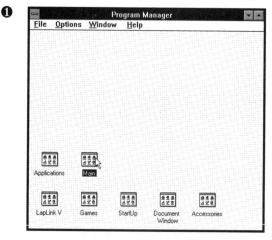

❷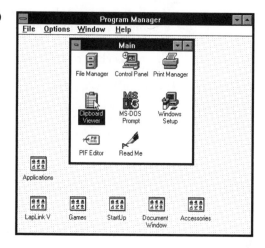

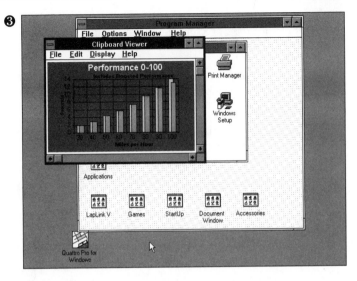

More stuff

The Clipboard can't always show exactly what you have cut or copied. If you copy a sound from the Windows Sound Recorder, for example, you just see a picture of a little microphone (the sound recorder icon) on the Clipboard. If you want to see what you're cutting, copying, and pasting, leave your Clipboard open at the bottom of the screen.

Most of the time, you use the Clipboard for temporary operations — cutting or copying information from one application and pasting it in another, for example — when there is no need to have it open all the time.

You can save the Clipboard's contents for later use. With the Clipboard open, do the following:

1. Click on File from the menu bar.

2. Click on Save As.

3. Type in a filename, and click on the OK command button or press Enter. Press Esc to leave the dialog box without saving anything.

Since the Clipboard is used for one-time operations, it can only hold one thing at a time. Every time you cut or copy material, the newly cut or copied material replaces any material that is in the Clipboard.

TIP

If Windows slows down after you cut or copy a large amount of information to the Clipboard (like a lot of text, pictures, or sounds, for example), it is because these kinds of operations can consume a lot of memory. Clearing the Clipboard after a large cut or copy is a very good idea, especially if your computer acts a little sluggish — like it just had a big meal:

1. Make sure you have the Clipboard viewer open.

2. Click on the Clipboard viewer application to make the application active.

3. Press the Del key to clear the Clipboard and let Windows use the memory for other applications.

Another way to clear the Clipboard is to cut or copy a single character to the Clipboard:

1. Highlight a single letter in a word processing application.

2. Press Ctrl+C.

Copying Program Items from One Group to Another

Used primarily for copying application icons from a window to a more frequently used group window.

You usually copy program items when you want a copy in the StartUp window so that the application starts automatically when Windows starts up.

To copy an application icon from one window to another, use the drag-and-drop method: Press and hold the Ctrl key. Then click and hold the left mouse button with the pointer on the application icon you want to copy. While still holding the mouse button, drag the application icon to the destination window. Let go of the mouse button to drop the copy of the application icon in its new home.

Steps

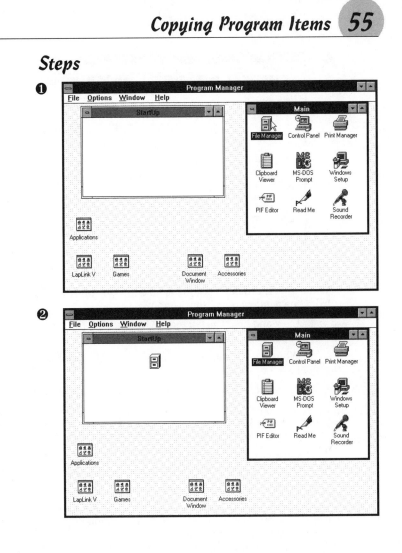

❸

Program Manager
<u>F</u>ile   <u>O</u>ptions   <u>W</u>indow   <u>H</u>elp

StartUp

File Manager

Main

File Manager   Control Panel   Print Manager

Clipboard Viewer   MS-DOS Prompt   Windows Setup

PIF Editor   Read Me   Sound Recorder

Applications

LapLink V   Games   Document Window   Accessories

More stuff

You may want to move, rather than copy, an application icon
from one window to another window:

1. Click and hold the left mouse button with the pointer on the
   application icon you want to move.

2. While holding the mouse button, drag the application icon
   to the destination window.

3. Let go of the mouse button to drop the application icon in
   the new window.

If, like me, you like to keep all of your ducks in a row, there is an
option in the Program Manager to fulfill your needs:

1. Click on Options in the Program Manager's menu bar.

2. Click on Auto Arrange. The check mark next to Auto
   Arrange means that it's on.

You can also move icons to another program group even if the
program group is minimized to an icon — if you don't care where
the icon is placed in the program group. Follow the steps for
copying a program item. Later, you can open the program group
to a window and tidy up.

Here's the keyboard shortcut for moving or copying an application icon:

1. Select the application icon by pressing Ctrl+Tab, Enter, and
   then the arrow key until the icon is selected.

2. Copy the application icon by pressing F8; move the
   application icon by pressing F7.

3. When the dialog box appears, press the up- or down-arrow
   keys to select the window you want to copy or move the
   application icon to.

4. After the correct window title is selected, press Enter; press Esc to get out of the dialog box without doing anything.

Creating a Group

Used for creating a window, referred to as a *program group,* for commonly used applications.

Click on File, New from the Program Manager's menu bar. Click on the Program Group radio button. Click on OK or press Enter to name a new program group; press Esc to make a quick exit without saving changes.

Steps

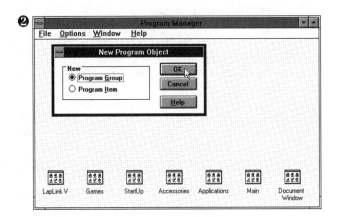

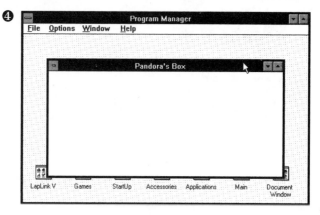

What It's Called	What It Does
Description	The text box where you type in the descriptive name that you want to appear in the group window's title bar and at the bottom of the program group icon in the Program Manager.
	Don't make the description too long, because when you turn a program group into an icon, a too-long title will rub elbows with the titles of other icons.
Group File	If you are creating a new group, this box is blank. If you leave the box blank, the Program Manager names the group file for you.
	Leaving this text box blank is definitely the best way to go. If you happen to be changing the properties of an existing group, the name of the group is in this box.

More stuff

Creating different program groups for different projects is like having a new folder for a project. Having too many program groups can slow Windows way down. If you have a lot of program group icons or windows, drag the application icons from several program groups into one program group and delete the empty program groups. Or keep most or all of the program groups minimized.

Ignore the Group File box. You can get into more trouble by filling it out for a new program group than by leaving it alone.

Creating a Program Item

Used to create an application icon for a program — usually a non-Windows program — that has never been installed for Windows before.

Open the window for the program group that you want to put the application icon into. Press and hold the Alt key while double-clicking inside the program group window. The Program Item Properties dialog box appears. Click on the Browse command button and select which program you want to have an application icon made for.

Steps

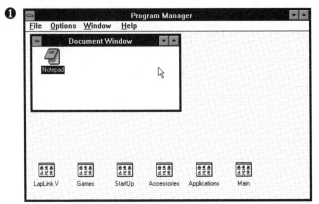

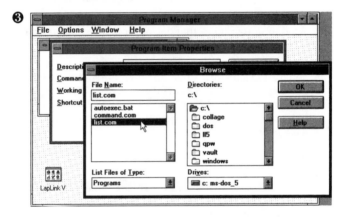

See the example in *Windows 3.1 For Dummies,* 2nd Edition, Chapter 11, "The Ever-Present Program Manager," and the example in *MORE Windows For Dummies*, Chapter 20, "Program Manager Keeps Loading Itself as an Icon!"

More stuff

What It's Called	What It Does
Description	The title that's going to show up below the group icon.
	This description is optional. If you leave the box blank, the Program Manager names the icon for you.

What It's Called	What It Does
Command Line	The place where you type the application's filename with any file extension — like TXT or DOC — and the path to the application, if necessary.
	If you can't remember all of the details exactly, use the Browse command button to open the Browse dialog box.
Working Directory	The place where you type the location of the application's user files and documents.
	This is optional. If you leave this text box blank, the application's directory becomes the working directory.
Shortcut Key	The place where you can assign a shortcut key combination to the application.
	You assign a shortcut key if you're into saving time and you frequently bring up a specific application. Whenever you press the three-key combination, the application starts a runnin'. A good keyboard combination is Ctrl+Shift+*first letter* of the application's name.
	Specifying a shortcut key is optional.
Run Minimized	Click on this check box if you want the application to open and run as a minimized icon on your desktop when you double-click the icon.
Change Icon	Brings up the Change Icon dialog box, where you can specify a different icon.
	Windows allows you a little creativity in the Change Icon dialog box, where you can replace the drab DOS icon for non-Windows applications.

You can't have more than 40 application icons in a window. Windows just won't let you. No ifs, ands, or buts.

Deleting a Group

Used when a program group is no longer needed for application icons.

To delete a group, the group you want to delete must be minimized to an icon. Click on the group and then press the Del key.
(You can't delete a program group as an icon when the group's
menu is sticking up above the program group icon. Press Esc to
get rid of the menu and then press Del.) Click on OK or press
Enter to get rid of the group icon; press Esc to exit without
deleting the icon.

When you delete a program group, you delete all the program and
application icons that are in it.

Steps

❸

| Program Manager | ▼ ▲ |

<u>F</u>ile   <u>O</u>ptions   <u>W</u>indow   <u>H</u>elp

LapLink V   Games   StartUp   Accessories   Applications   Main   Document Window

More stuff

Click on the group icon that you want to delete, or from the Program Manager menu bar, click on File, Delete. A confirmation dialog box pops up asking if you're sure you want to delete the highlighted icon. Press Enter to delete the group or press Esc to abort the whole operation.

When the group icon is deleted — and all of the application icons with it — the data files for the application icons within the group are not deleted from the hard disk.

Another, safer, way to delete a group is to delete all of the application icons inside the group and then delete the group itself. If you delete all of the application icons from within the group first, you don't have to reduce the group to an icon to delete it (see "Deleting a Program Item" in this section); just press Del when you've got the empty program group in your sights.

Here is the keyboard shortcut: press Ctrl+Tab or Ctrl+F6 to move to the group that you want to delete and then press Del to remove the group icon from the face of the Program Manager.

Windows will delete a program group even if it's full of application icons. Make sure that you're not deleting a whole program group when you really mean to just delete one of the application icons inside of it. If you goof and delete a program group by accident, you have to go through the whole process of creating the group and the application icons from scratch. Deleting a Program Item

Deleting a Program Item

Used when you don't want an application icon to reference a program on your hard disk anymore.

Open the group window that contains the icon you want to delete. Select the program icon for the item by either clicking on it or using the arrow keys. Press the Del key. Click on OK in the warning dialog box or press Enter to vanquish the application icon from the Program Manager; press Esc to make a quick exit without deleting the program item.

Steps

❶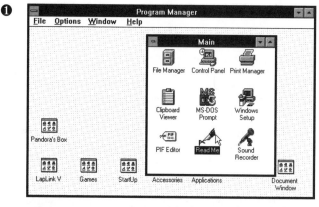

❷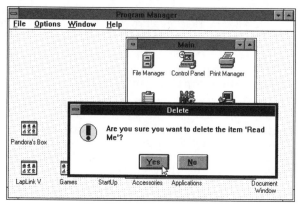

❸

Program Manager

File   Options   Window   Help

Main

File Manager Control Panel Print Manager

Clipboard   MS-DOS   Windows
Viewer   Prompt   Setup

Pandora's Box

PIF Editor   Sound
             Recorder

LapLink V   Games   StartUp   Accessories   Applications   Document
                                                            Window

More stuff

Here's the keyboard shortcut: from the Program Manager
window, press Alt, F, D.

TIP

Deleting an application icon does not delete the program from
your hard disk.

REFERENCE

See "Deleting Files and Directories" in Part IV, "File Manager," to
quench that destructive thirst you may have.

MS-DOS Prompt

Used to start a full-screen or windowed DOS session.

Double-click on the red, purple, and yellow DOS icon in the Main
program group.

Steps

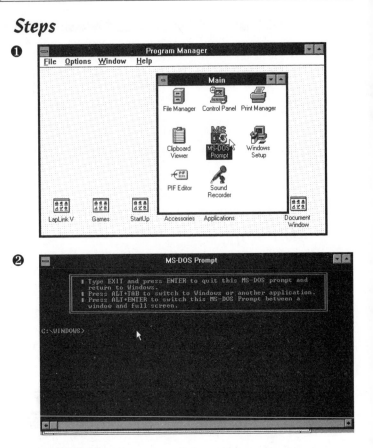

❶ (Program Manager — Main window showing File Manager, Control Panel, Print Manager, Clipboard Viewer, MS-DOS Prompt, Windows Setup, PIF Editor, Sound Recorder)

❷ (MS-DOS Prompt window)

More stuff

You can only run DOS in a window if Windows is running in 386 Enhanced mode.

See "Windows Modes" in Part I, "Windows Basics," to find out the difference between Standard mode and pie a la mode.

Alt+Enter is a neat way to toggle between a DOS window and a DOS full-screen session. If you can't get out of a full-screen DOS session, you may not be in 386 Enhanced mode, even if you are running on a 386 or 486 computer.

A DOS window is the only place that you can transfer information between non-Windows applications and Windows applications. (See "Transferring Information between Applications" in Part II, "Application Basics").

Don't run these commands at the DOS prompt: Chkdsk /f, Fdisk, Recover, Select, Format C:

See the examples in *Windows 3.1 For Dummies,* 2nd Edition, Chapter 22, "Ten DOS Commands You Shouldn't Run under Windows,"and the example in *MORE Windows For Dummies*, Chapter 6, "DOS Commands to Avoid While You Are Running Windows."

Opening a Group Window

Used to start an application from a group.

Open a group window that has an application icon that you want to start. To open a group window, double-click the group icon representing the program group that you want to open, or press Enter when the icon is selected.

Steps

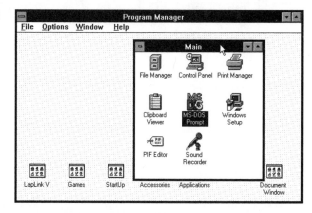

More stuff

On the Program Manager's menu bar, click on Window and press the number that corresponds to the group that you want to open.

Once the application is running, you can either shrink the group window to an icon by clicking on the minimize button or you can just leave the group window alone.

 See "Parts of a Window" in Part I, "Windows Basics," if you don't know the difference between a minimize button and miniature golf.

PIF Editor

Used to work on files containing information that Windows needs to work well with non-Windows applications.

From the Program Manager, double-click on the Main group icon. Double-click on the PIF Editor application icon.

Steps

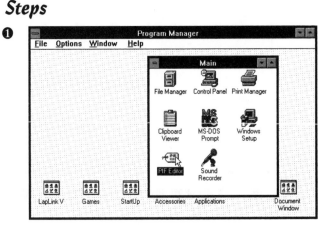

❷

```
┌─────────────── Program Manager ──────────── ▼ ▲ ┐
│ File   Options   Window   Help                   │
│ ┌──────────── PIF Editor - [Untitled] ──── ▼ ▲ ┐ │
│ │ File   Mode   Help                          │ │
│ │ Program Filename:  ▷ [                    ]  │ │
│ │ Window Title:      [                      ]  │ │
│ │ Optional Parameters: [                    ]  │ │
│ │ Start-up Directory:  [                    ]  │ │
│ │ Video Memory:  ◉ Text  ○ Low Graphics  ○ High Graphics │ │
│ │ Memory Requirements:  KB Required [128]  KB Desired [640] │ │
│ │ EMS Memory:   KB Required [0]   KB Limit [1024] │ │
│ │ XMS Memory:   KB Required [0]   KB Limit [1024] │ │
│ │ Display Usage: ◉ Full Screen   Execution: ☐ Background │ │
│ │               ○ Windowed                  ☐ Exclusive │ │
│ │ ☒ Close Window on Exit    [Advanced...]   │ Document │ │
│ │                                           │ Window │ │
│ │ Press F1 for Help on Program Filename.      │ │
│ └─────────────────────────────────────────────┘ │
└──────────────────────────────────────────────────┘
```

This is the 386 Enhanced mode PIF Editor.

What It's Called	*What It Does*
Program Filename	The place where you type in the drive and path for the program you want to tweak.
	Use File, Open from the menu bar to work on an existing PIF file.
Window Title	The place where you get to be creative and name the program.
	What you type here shows up in the non-Windows application title bar when the application is running. If you leave this box blank, the title bar displays the application file without an extension.
Optional Parameters	Type anything here that you would normally type after the filename if you were to run it in DOS.
	If your non-Windows application does not need any parameters, you can leave this box blank.
	If you want Windows to ask you for parameters when you start the application, you can type a question mark here.
Start-up Directory	Leave this box blank unless you want your non-Windows application to save files someplace other than where it starts from.

(continues)

What It's Called	*What It Does*
Video Memory	Contains three options — Text, Low Graphics, and High Graphics — that tell Windows what kind of non-Windows graphics requirements your application needs.
	If your application is having problems being displayed properly, you can click on a different radio button and see what happens.
Memory Requirements	Best left to a Windows guru.
EMS Memory	Best left to a Windows guru.
XMS Memory	Best left to a Windows guru.
Display Usage	Click on one of these radio buttons to start your non-Windows application in a window or in full-screen.
	Running in a window uses more memory than running in full-screen mode, and it can slow down your non-Windows application. Having your non-Windows application in a window lets you cut, copy, and paste between applications. You can also switch between full-screen and a window by pressing Alt+Enter.

See "Transferring Information between Applications" in Part II, "Application Basics," to get away from using scissors, a Xerox machine, and glue around your monitor.

Execution	Check out "Changing the Settings for Running a Non-Windows Application" in Part II, "Application Basics."
Advanced options	Best left to a Windows guru.

For information about EMS memory, XMS memory, memory requirements, and advanced options, see IDG's *Windows 3.1 SECRETS*.

More stuff

PIF — rhymes with *whiff* — is an acronym for Program Information File.

When you create an application icon for a non-Windows application, Windows automatically creates a PIF if the non-Windows application doesn't already have one. When you double-click on a non-Windows application to start it, Windows goes out to look for a PIF for that application.

If by chance the default Windows PIF called — what else — _DEFAULT.PIF doesn't work with your non-Windows application, you can always modify _DEFAULT.PIF or (if you really feel like getting your hands dirty) you can create a new PIF for your non-Windows application.

The only change you would really want to make to _DEFAULT.PIF is to click on the Window check box in the Display Usage section. This makes all your non-Windows applications that use _DEFAULT.PIF start in a window. You have to be running in 386 Enhanced mode for this to work.

See "Windows Modes" in Part I, "Windows Basics," to get the scoop on modes.

Reducing a Group Window to an Icon

Used if there are too many open windows inside the Program Manager.

To reduce a group window to an icon, click on the minimize button.

Steps

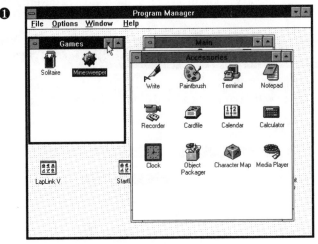

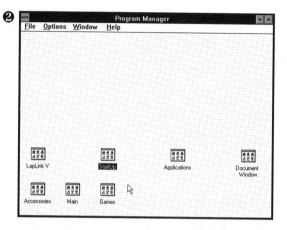

More stuff

For you keyboard jockeys, press Alt+-(hyphen) to open the control menu for the group and use the down-arrow key to choose Minimize; then press Enter. You can also double-click on the control menu button, which is in the upper left-hand corner of the group icon window. Closing a group window actually shrinks the group window to an icon at the bottom of the Program Manager; it doesn't really close it. Strange, huh?

Windows Setup

Used to change the computer's settings, set up applications to use with Windows, and add or remove parts of Windows.

Steps

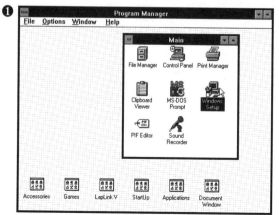

Options	Command
Change System Settings	Lets you change the kind of video display (including colors and size), keyboard, or mouse you have, or lets you get Windows ready for a network connection.
	Click on the downward-pointing arrow of the option that you want to change (or press Alt+down arrow). When you find the setting that you want, click on it.
Set Up Applications	One of the easiest ways to set up an application for Windows.
	See the example in *Windows 3.1 For Dummies,* 2nd Edition, Chapter 11, "Putting a Favorite Program's Icon into the Program Manager."
Add/Remove Windows Components	Primarily used to remove non-essential Windows components to gain disk space. You will probably never find yourself here unless your hard disk is scratching at the door of being completely full.
	Click the check boxes beside what you want Windows to remove, or click on the Files command button to remove individual components. Windows tells you how much space you'll save. Press Enter to delete such non-essentials as Solitaire and Minesweeper — NOT! Press Esc to save yourself from deleting all of the games Windows has to offer.

See the example in *Windows 3.1 For Dummies*, 2nd Edition, Chapter 10, "Playing with New Video Modes."

More stuff

Get those Windows installation disks out if you plan to mess with any options in the Windows Setup box.

If you want to use Set Up Applications, follow these steps:

1. After you click on Set Up Applications, a Setup Applications dialog box appears.

2. Check that Search for application is selected and press Enter.

3. Click on the drive that you want searched.

4. Click on the Search Now command button or press Enter.

   Windows searches for applications and presents the search results to you.

5. Click on the application names that you want to add or click on the Add All command button to select all of the applications that Windows finds.

6. Click on the OK command button or press Enter to create icons for those applications that you selected.

You have to exit and restart Windows to put into effect any options that you changed in Windows Setup.

Part IV:
File Manager

Arranging Directory Windows

Allows a user to have all open directory windows within the File Manager neatly visible, with no overlap.

Click on Window from the File Manager menu bar. Then click on the Tile option.

Steps

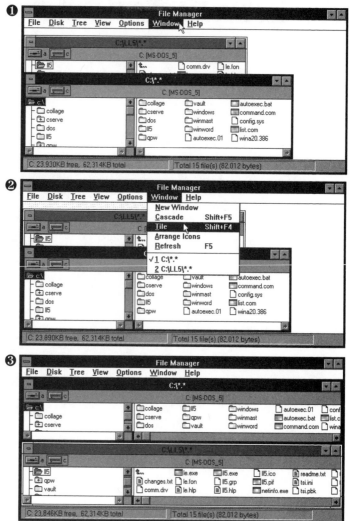

Option	What It Does
Cascade	Arranges directory windows by making them the same size and then overlapping them so that only the title bar is showing. (See "Parts of a Directory Window" later in this section for an explanation of title bars.)
	The cascade arrangement makes the open directory windows look like you just neatly spread out a deck of cards.
	You also can press Shift+F5 from within the File Manager workspace to start the Cascade command.
Tile	Arranges directory windows by making the windows small enough so that they fit neatly next to each other and then arranges them in a tile pattern.
	This command makes all the open windows look like neat little tiles on a kitchen countertop. The more windows you have open, the more tiles you have.
	If you select Window, Tile from the File Manager menu bar, the directory windows arrange themselves vertically (one on top of the other).
	If you press and hold down the Shift key while selecting Tile, the directory windows arrange themselves horizontally (side by side).
	You also can press Shift+F4 from within the File Manager workspace to arrange the directory windows horizontally.

More stuff

The Tile and Cascade commands only deal with arranging open directory windows.

Associating Files with Their Applications

Used to load an application and a data or document file in one fell swoop.

File Manager allows you to associate a particular data or document file with an application so that instead of starting an application and then loading a data or document file, you can just double-click on a data or document file, and File Manager opens the application as well.

Click on File, Associate from the Program Manager's menu bar. The Associate dialog box appears. Type the extension of the file or files that you want to associate with a particular application in the Files with Extensions box. In the Associate With list box, double-click on the application that you want the file or files associated with. Click on the OK command button or press Enter to save this file extension association; press the Esc key to exit without associating a file with an application.

After you associate a particular file or set of files with an application, whenever you double-click on the filename with that particular extension, the application starts automatically.

Steps

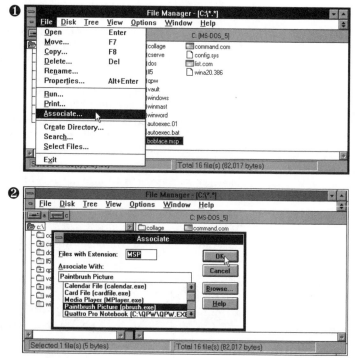

 See the example in *Windows 3.1 For Dummies*, 2nd Edition, Chapter 12, "Telling Windows What Program Made What File."

More stuff

The file icon changes to a document file icon when it is associated with an application.

If you're looking for a particular application to associate to and you don't find it, you can use the Browse command button to bring up the Browse dialog box, where you can search for the unlisted application.

Many Windows applications get associated with a particular filename extension when you install the application. The Associate With list box shows all the applications that registered with the Windows concierge when the applications were installed.

TIP

If you load a particular document or data file frequently — a document or data file that already has an application association — you can put the file itself in a group window. This is the easiest shortcut for opening a document or data file with an application, and it will only work if you don't rename or move the document or data file in the future.

1. Find the document or data file in the File Manager that you want to create a total shortcut for.

2. Open the group window that you want this document or data file shortcut to reside in.

3. Have both the File Manager and the group window open so that you can see inside both of them.

4. Click and hold the left mouse button on the document or data file and drag the file to the group window.

5. Let go of the mouse button.

   The file turns into an icon that represents the application that it is associated with and has the filename underneath the icon.

Now you can double-click on the new icon to start the application and load the document or data file!

Changing Directories

Used when you want to see or work with files in a different directory or subdirectory than you currently see in the directory contents section of the directory window.

On the left-hand side of the directory window is the directory tree, which has a rectangle around the current directory. On the right-hand side of the directory window is the directory's contents, containing the subdirectories and files that are in that directory (you can liken these to documents within a manila folder).

On the left-hand side of the directory window, click on the directory whose contents you want to view. Use the scroll bars to move up and down the directory tree.

Steps

❶
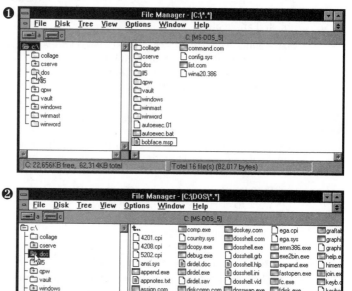

❷

See the example in *Windows 3.1 For Dummies*, 2nd Edition, Chapter 12, "Peering into Your Drives and Directories."

More stuff

In the directory contents side of the directory window, if you click on the up arrow (which looks like a bent arrow with two dots beside it), you move up one directory level unless you're at the root directory. If you're at the root directory, the up arrow disappears.

Here are the keyboard shortcuts:

Press This	To Do This
Ctrl+Down arrow	Show the next directory at the same level, if one exists.
Ctrl+Up arrow	Show the previous directory at the same level, if one exists.
Home or backslash	Show the root directory.

Press This	To Do This
Left arrow or Backspace	Show the next directory level up from the current directory, if one exists.
PgDn	Show the directory one screen down from the current directory, if one exists.
PgUp	Show the directory one screen up from the current directory, if one exists.
Right arrow	Show the first subdirectory of the current directory.
Up arrow or down arrow	Show the directory above or below the current directory, if one exists.
Character	Show the next directory that begins with that letter or number that is selected.

See the shortcut keys in Part VII.

Changing Drives

Used when you want to view the contents of another drive.

The current drive icon has a rectangle around it. To the right of the current drive icon is the drive letter and its name (referred to as a *volume*). The directory window, which is underneath the drive icon, shows the directories, subdirectories, and files of the current drive.

Change to a different drive by single-clicking on a different drive icon.

Steps

①

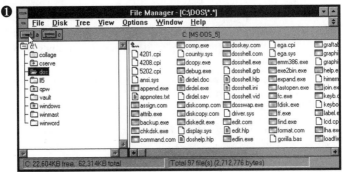

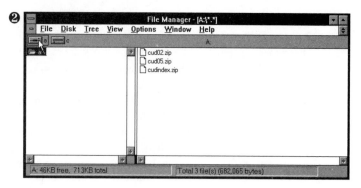

More stuff

If you double-click instead of single-click on a drive icon, you open a new directory window that gives you information on the newly selected drive. But you still have a directory window of the last drive you looked at.

The File Manager also allows you to choose a different drive by double-clicking on the background area where the drive icons are located. When the Select Drive dialog box appears, double-click on the drive you want to change to.

When you are changing drives, the File Manager searches the newly selected drive to display the directories, subdirectories, and files, which can take a bit of time to accomplish. You can press the Esc key to stop File Manager from doing the search, but then only a partial directory is displayed. You can press the F5 key to search the drive completely.

If you usually view the contents of floppy disks and you find yourself clicking on the drive icon every time you put a new disk in, you probably wish there were a better way. Well, there is.

1. Put a floppy disk in the drive.
2. Single-click on the drive icon representing the floppy drive.
3. Take the floppy disk out of the drive and insert a new one.
4. Press the F5 key. A listing of the new floppy's contents appears.

You can also use the F5 key to refresh the directory window view on the current drive.

See the shortcut keys in Part VII.

Changing File Attributes

Used to change file attributes to or from archive, hidden, read only, or system.

To change the file attributes for a single file, click on the file that you want to change attributes for. From the menu bar, click on File, Properties. The Properties dialog box appears. Click on the check box in the Attributes area that you want to select or deselect. Click on the OK command button or press Enter when done; press Esc to exit without making changes.

Steps

❶

File Manager - [C:*.*]

File   Disk   Tree   View   Options   Window   Help

C: [MS-DOS_5]

Open	Enter
Move...	F7
Copy...	F8
Delete...	Del
Rename...	
Properties...	Alt+Enter
Run...	
Print...	
Associate...	
Create Directory...	
Search...	
Select Files...	
Exit	

qpw
vault
windows
winmast
winword
autoexec.01   a
autoexec.bat   a
bobface.msp   a
command.com   a
config.sys   a
list.com   a
wina20.386   a

Total 16 file(s) (82,017 bytes)

❷

File Manager - [C:*.*]

File   Disk   Tree   View   Options   Window   Help

C: [MS-DOS_5]

qpw

Properties for BOBFACE.MSP

File Name:	BOBFACE.MSP	OK
Size:	5 bytes	Cancel
Last Change:	9/7/90 7:34:42AM	Help
Path:	C:\	

Attributes
☒ Read Only   ☐ Hidden
☒ Archive   ☐ System

Selected 1 file(s) (5 bytes)   Total 16 file(s) (82,017 bytes)

❸

```
                    File Manager - [C:\*.*]
 □  File   Disk   Tree   View   Options   Window   Help
 ▭ a  ▭ c                    C: [MS-DOS_5]
 📁 c:\                    📁 qpw
  ├─ 📁 collage            📁 vault
  ├─ 📁 cserve             📁 windows
  ├─ 📁 dos                📁 winmast
  ├─ 📁 ll5                📁 winword
  ├─ 📁 qpw                📄 autoexec.01        a
  ├─ 📁 vault              📄 autoexec.bat       a
  ├─ 📁 windows            📄 bobface.msp        ra
  ├─ 📁 winmast            📄 command.com        a
  └─ 📁 winword            📄 config.sys         a
                          📄 list.com           a
                          📄 wina20.386         a
 Selected 1 file(s) (5 bytes)      Total 16 file(s) (82,017 bytes)
```

Option	What It Does
Read Only	Makes a file so you can look at it but not change it.
	If you have files that you use as reference files and you don't change them or don't want them changed, you can make them read only.
Archive	Lets you know that the file has been modified since it was last backed up. No harm, no foul, just leave it alone.
Hidden	If you can see these files in the File Manager, you probably have the Show Hidden/System Files checked in the By File Type dialog box.
	This attribute hides the file from your prying eyes in the File Manager and from a DIR at the DOS prompt. These files are marked hidden for a reason, so don't play with them.
System	Marks a file as a DOS system file.
	If you can see these files in the File Manager, you probably have the Show Hidden/System Files checked in the By File Type dialog box.
	These files let you boot up your computer, so don't delete, move, change, or play with them. Just say No.

More stuff

If you're really itching to see file attributes, you can click on View, All File Details from the File Manager menu bar. You can also use View, Partial Details from the menu bar and check the File Attributes check box.

Changing File Manager Options

Used to change the way the File Manager displays or handles directories, subdirectories, and files.

Steps

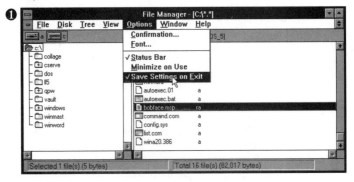

Option	What It Does
Confirmation	When on, displays confirmation messages asking whether you are sure you want to carry out specific operations such as file delete, directory delete, file replacement, mouse actions (copying and moving files with the mouse, for example), and disk commands (like format or copy disk).
	This is an important option and all check boxes within this option should be checked if they aren't already. If any of the check boxes in the Confirmation dialog box are not checked, check them and click on the OK command button.
	Here's the keyboard shortcut: from the File Manager, press Alt, O, C.
Font	Brings up a dialog box allowing you to change the fonts that the File Manager displays.
	Here's the keyboard shortcut: from the File Manager, press Alt, O, F.
Status Bar	Displays file information at the bottom of the directory window.
	A check mark next to the command means it's on.

(continues)

Option	What It Does
	Here's the keyboard shortcut: from the File Manager, press Alt, O, S.
Minimize on Use	Shrinks the File Manager window to an icon whenever you start an application. The File Manager icon resides on the bottom of the desktop.
	A check mark next to the command means it's on.
	Here's the keyboard shortcut: from the File Manager, press Alt, O, M.
Save Setting on Exit	Saves the order of the windows and the views (minimized or maximized, for example) of open directories in File Manager when you exit File Manager.
	A check mark next to the command means it's on.
	Here's the keyboard shortcut: from the File Manager, press Alt, O, E.

See "Fonts" in Part V, "Control Panel," for more on fonts.

Changing the Information Displayed in a Directory Window

Used to view only the tree information, directory information, or both; used to view just the filename, partial file details, or all file details; and used to change the sort order of files by date, name, size, or type and to determine whether files and directories are listed alphabetically.

Steps

Option	What It Does
Tree and Directory	This command shows the directory tree on the left side of the split bar and the file contents on the right in the directory window. A check mark next to the command means it's on.
	Here's the keyboard shortcut: from the File Manager, press Alt, V, R.
Tree Only	This command shows only the directory tree in the directory window. A check mark next to the command means it's on.
	Here's the keyboard shortcut: from the File Manager, press Alt, V, O.
Directory Only	Shows only the directory contents in the directory window. A check mark next to the command means it's on.
	Here's the keyboard shortcut: from the File Manager, press Alt, V, O.
Split	No, this doesn't mean that the File Manager's going to take a powder. When you select this command, you can use the mouse or the left- and right-arrow keys to show more of the directory tree or more of the file contents by moving the split bar.
	Press the mouse button or press Enter when you have the right ratio of tree to file contents in the directory window. If you change your mind while you are moving the split bar, press the Esc key.
	You need to have both the directory tree and the directory contents visible in the directory window for this to work. *(continues)*

Option	What It Does
	Here's the keyboard shortcut: from the File Manager, press Alt, V, L.
Name	Shows only the name of the files in the directory window. A check mark next to the command means it's on.
	Here's the keyboard shortcut: from the File Manager, press Alt, V, N.
All File Details	Shows the whole enchilada, including attributes, name, size, and last modification date and time, when you view file details in the directory window. A check mark next to the command means it's on.
	Here's the keyboard shortcut: from the File Manager, press Alt, V, A.
Partial Details	Shows the name of the files in the directory window; also can show attributes, last modification date, last modification time, or file size. A check mark next to the command means it's on.
	Here's the keyboard shortcut: from the File Manager, press Alt, V, P.
Sort by Name	Alphabetically sorts the directories and the files in the directory window, *Abe* being at the top and *Ziggy* being at the bottom. A check mark next to the command means it's on.
	Here's the keyboard shortcut: from the File Manager, press Alt, V, S.
Sort by Type	Alphabetically sorts the directories and the files in the directory window by extension. Sorts directories first. A check mark next to the command means it's on.
	Here's the keyboard shortcut: from the File Manager, press Alt, V, B.
Sort by Size	Sorts the files in the directory window by putting the biggest on top and smallest at the very bottom. These guys really know how to dog pile! A check mark next to the command means it's on.
	Here's the keyboard shortcut: from the File Manager, press Alt, V, Z.

Option	*What It Does*
Sort by Date	Sorts the files in the directory window by last modification date, with today being at the top and last year being farther down the pile. A check mark next to the command means it's on.
	To use this option, you need a working computer clock.
	Here's the keyboard shortcut: from the File Manager, press Alt, V, D.
By File Type	Shows the group of files that you have selected (either directories, documents, applications, or other files). You can also show only those types of files that suit your needs.
	This is pretty heavy stuff and you may just want to leave every option at default.
	Here's the keyboard shortcut: from the File Manager, press Alt, V, T.

More stuff

The file details, name, and partial details commands in the View pull-down menu only affect the active directory window.

If you want to save your settings after you have all of your options just right, click on Options, Save Settings on Exit. Make sure this setting has a check mark next to it. But if you want these settings as a default, call up File Manager again and then uncheck Save Settings on Exit. This holds your custom settings in the File Manager.

Copying a Disk

Used to make a copy of a 5¼-inch or a 3½-inch disk.

Here is how you copy an entire disk with only one floppy drive in your computer. To copy the entire disk, insert the disk that you want to copy information from (called the *source disk*) in the disk drive. Click on Disk, Copy Disk from the File Manager menu bar. A confirmation dialog box asking whether you're sure you want to copy the whole disk shows up on the scene. Press Enter. Another dialog box asking you to insert the disk appears. Since you already put the disk in, click on the OK command button or press Enter. Another dialog box appears, giving you the percentage of the disk that has been copied. When the computer asks you to swap disks, do so. Press the Esc key at any time to stop the process.

Steps

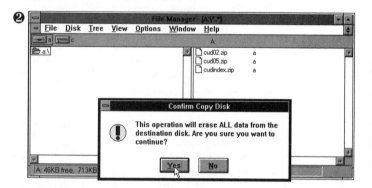

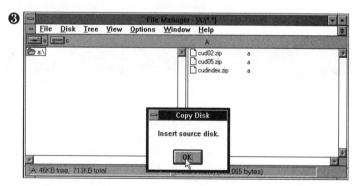

See the example in *Windows 3.1 For Dummies*, 2nd Edition, Chapter 12, "Copying a Disk," and the example in *MORE Windows For Dummies*, Chapter 2, "Copy files from a floppy disk to the hard drive."

More stuff

When you copy a floppy disk, both disks must have the same
storage capacity. For example, if the disk you are copying from is
a 720K, 3½-inch disk (low-density, coaster size disk), the disk you
copy to must be the same capacity and size.

If you're not using the 3½-inch disks, don't forget to close the door
on the front of the drive when you put the disks in.

If your computer has two floppy disk drives, a dialog box appears
asking for the source drive (the drive you want to copy from) and
the destination drive (which drive you want to copy to). The
source drive is usually drive A, and the destination drive is
usually drive B. Click on the OK command button after you specify.

Copying Files and Directories

Used to make a copy of files or directories from the hard disk to a
floppy disk or vice versa.

Steps

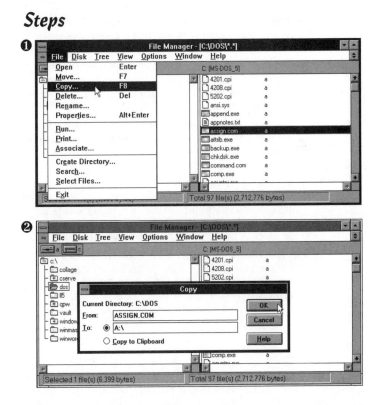

More stuff

You can also copy files and directories by just dragging and dropping them with the mouse.

If you are copying the file from one part of a drive to another or from one directory to another on the same drive, you have to press and hold down the Ctrl key while you use the mouse to drag the file.

If you are copying a directory, the directory, all of its subdirectories, and all files are copied also.

If you are copying files to a different directory on the same disk drive, the place you are copying to can be a drive icon, directory icon, or directory window.

1. Be sure that the window you are copying from and the window that you are copying to are visible in the File Manager workspace.
2. If you are copying files to a drive icon, the files go into the current directory in the drive icon.
3. Press and hold down the Ctrl key.
4. Press and hold down the mouse button and drag the file to where you want to copy it. (A plus sign appears on the file to show that you are copying the file and not moving it.)
5. Let go of the mouse button when you get to where you want to copy the file.

   A confirmation dialog box shows up asking whether you are sure that you want to copy the file.
6. Click on the Yes command button or press the Enter key to copy the file; click on the No command button if you don't want to copy the file.

If you are copying a file to a file with the same name, a dialog box appears asking whether you are sure you want to copy over the file. The names, sizes, and time/date stamp are next to the files in the dialog box so that you can check whether you really want to overwrite the file. Click on the Yes button if you want to overwrite the file, or click on the No button to leave the file alone.

If you are copying multiple files and you reach this dialog box, and you are sure that you want to copy over the files, you can click on the Yes to All command button. The Yes to All command button allows you the luxury of not having to click on a Yes command button a zillion times.

If you want to copy more than one file:

1. Click on the first file that you want to copy.
2. Press and hold down the Shift key.
3. Click on the last file that you want to copy. When you click on the last file, all of the files between the first and the last files become highlighted.

   If you want more files in the highlighted list, hold down the Ctrl key as you select more individual files. By holding down the Ctrl key, you may also unselect from the highlighted list by clicking on them.
4. Release the Shift key.
5. Click and hold down on the left mouse button on the bottom of the selection you have just made.
6. Drag the files to where you want them to go.
7. Let go of the mouse button.

You can also use the keyboard to copy a file (although why you would want to do so is questionable).

1. Press the F8 function key or press Alt, F, C. A dialog box appears.
2. Type in the filename that you want to copy in the From box. If the file that you want to copy is not in the directory listed in the Current Directory portion of the dialog box, type in the directory before the filename.
3. Press the Tab key to move to the To: box.
4. Type in the destination (where you want the file to go), including the subdirectory and drive letter if needed. Type in the filename.
5. Press the Tab key until you reach the OK command button. Press the Enter key to copy the file or press the Esc key to abort the whole operation.

Creating a Directory

Used to make a new directory to hold applications, documents, or data files.

Click on the Root directory with the left mouse button. Click on File, Create Directory from the File Manager menu bar. A Create Directory dialog box shows up. Type in the name of the new directory. Click on the OK command button or press the Enter key to keep the new directory name. Press the Esc key to exit without naming or making a new directory.

Steps

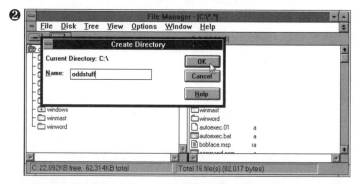

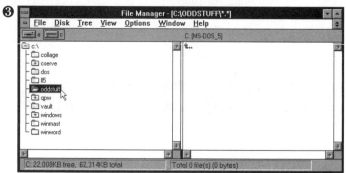

More stuff

You can now copy or move files or directories to your newly created directory.

It's best for a directory name (or a filename for that matter) not to have any more than eight characters. Just keeping around eight is a good idea. The name itself must start with either a letter or number, and it can contain any upper- or lowercase characters except

the period (.)
the slash (/)
the bracket ([)
the semicolon (;)
the equals sign (=)
a quotation mark (")
the backslash (\)
the colon (:)
the vertical bar (|)
or the comma (,)

The name cannot contain any spaces or use any of the following names, which are reserved and cannot be used for files and directories:

CON
AUX
COM1
COM2
COM3
COM4
LPT1
LPT2
LPT3
PRN
NUL

If you use these characters or names in a directory or file, some funky things can occur.

Examples of valid names: MISSILE, snipe, DEFCON1, MYGAME, FRIDOC, TOADLINE, 1FATCOW, TOE2TOE, bobshark, Xingu, tachYON, NoID, REbus, Red_Burn ... well, you get the idea.

Deleting Files and Directories

Used when a file or directory is no longer needed.

Click on the file or directory you want to delete. Click on File, Delete from the File Manager menu bar or press the Del key. When the Delete dialog box shows up, click on the OK command button. The Confirm Delete dialog box appears. Click on the OK command button or press the Enter key to delete the directory or file. Press the Esc key or click on the Cancel command button to exit without deleting anything.

Steps

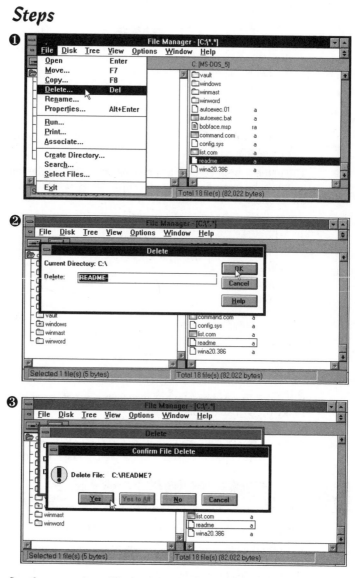

See the example in *Windows 3.1 For Dummies*, 2nd Edition, Chapter 12, "Deleting and Undeleting Files."

More stuff

You can also press the Del key when a file or directory is high-lighted to delete the file or directory.

If you are deleting more than one file or directory and you do not want to confirm each and every deletion, you can choose the Yes to All command button to have the File Manager delete all of the files in one fell swoop.

If you delete a directory that is not empty, all files and sub-directories in that directory are deleted.

 Be extremely careful when you are deleting files or directories, even if you're running DOS Version 5 or 6 or have a file recovery application of some type. If you have accidentally deleted a file or directory, don't do anything else, grab the nearest Windows guru and ask him to help you with the Undelete command. Or see the *DOS For Dummies Quick Reference* for details on how to use the Undelete command.

Expanding and Collapsing Directory Levels

Used to see or hide subdirectories and files within subdirectories.

To expand a directory, double-click on the directory, or select it and press Enter. To collapse a directory, double-click on the directory you want to collapse.

Steps

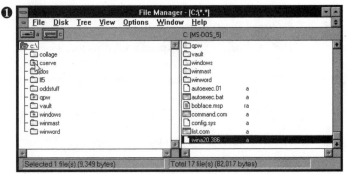

❷

```
                    File Manager - [C:\CSERVE\*.*]
 □  File  Disk  Tree  View  Options  Window  Help
 [▭] a [▭] c                        C: [MS-DOS_5]
┌─────────────────────────────┐ ┌──────────────────────────────┐
│ 📁 c:\                        │ │ 📁 ...                        │
│  ├ 📁 collage                 │ │  📁 download                  │
│  ├ 📁 cserve                  │ │  📁 fcabinet                  │
│  │  ├ 📁 download             │ │  📁 gif                       │
│  │  ├ 📁 fcabinet             │ │  📁 scripts                   │
│  │  ├ 📁 gif                  │ │  📁 support                   │
│  │  ├ 📁 scripts              │ │  📁 wincim                    │
│  │  ├ 📁 support              │ │  📁 winsign                   │
│  │  ├ 📁 wincim               │ │  📄 cis.ini          a        │
│  │  └ 📁 winsign              │ │  📄 readme.txt       a        │
│  ├ 📁 dos                     │ │                               │
│  ├ 📁 ll5                     │ │                               │
│  └ 📁 addstuff                │ │                               │
└─────────────────────────────┘ └──────────────────────────────┘
 C: 21,806KB free, 62,314KB total    Total 9 file(s) (4,487 bytes)
```

More stuff

When you expand a directory, the names of the directory branches are displayed next to the folder icons which represent the directories.

If you keep clicking on the root directory, all of the subdirectories collapse into the root directory icon. Just double-click on the root directory to expand the branches again.

If you want to display whether a directory has nested directories within it, click on Tree, Indicate Expandable Branches from the menu bar (or press Alt, T, I). When this command is active (a check mark appears beside it), a plus sign shows up inside the directory icon, indicating whether the directory contains subdirectories. A minus sign inside the directory icon indicates that the directory has been fully expanded and doesn't have any more directories to show.

This

Keyboard Shortcut	Does This
The + key or Alt, T, X	Expands one directory level
The * key or Alt, T, B	Expands a branch of a directory
Ctrl+* or Alt, T, A	Expands all of the branches
The - (hyphen) key or Alt, T, C	Collapses a branch

Formatting a Disk

Prepares a blank disk so that it can accept files.

Be very careful when you format a disk because formatting a disk wipes out any files that are on the disk.

Steps

Option	What It Does
Disk In	Specifies the drive that contains the floppy disk that you want to format: A or B.
Capacity	Specifies the capacity of the disk that you are about to format. You can choose between high and double density.
Label	The place where you put in the name for the disk, up to 11 characters. Go ahead and be creative with this one.
Make System Disk	Copies the system files to the formatted disk so that you can boot from the disk.
Quick Format	Performs a quick format of a previously formatted disk.

More stuff

If you're using DOS Version 5 or later and you reformat a floppy disk that has valuable data on it, you may be able to recover at least most of the file, using the UNFORMAT command. However, you must use this command before you put any new files on the disk. See the *DOS For Dummies Quick Reference* for details on use of this command.

Moving Files and Directories

Used to move files or directories from the hard disk to a floppy disk and remove them from the hard disk or vice versa.

Steps

❷

```
┌─────────────────────── File Manager - [C:\CSERVE\*.*] ──────────────────┐
│  File   Disk   Tree   View   Options   Window   Help                     │
├──────────────────────────────────────────────────────────────────────── │
│  ▭ a  ▭ c                       C: [MS-DOS_5]                             │
│  ┌ c:\                                    ┌ t...                          │
│  ├ ▭ collage                              ├ ▭ download                    │
│  ├ ▭ cserve                               └ ▭ fcabinet                    │
│  ├─┌ do┌──────────────────── Move ──────────────────────────┐           │
│  │ ├ fca│                                             ┌────────┐          │
│  │ ├ gif│ Current Directory: C:\CSERVE                │   OK   │          │
│  │ ├ scr│                                             └────────┘          │
│  │ ├ sup│ From:    README.TXT                         ┌────────┐          │
│  │ ├ win│                                             │ Cancel │          │
│  │ └ win│ To:      C:\                                └────────┘          │
│  ├ ▭ dos│                                             ┌────────┐          │
│  ├ ▭ II5│                                             │  Help  │          │
│  └ ▭ ado└─────────────────────────────────────────────────────┘         │
├──────────────────────────────────────────────────────────────────────── │
│ Selected 1 file(s) (3,584 bytes)        Total 9 file(s) (4,487 bytes)    │
└──────────────────────────────────────────────────────────────────────────┘
```

More stuff

You can also move files and directories by dragging and dropping them with the mouse. If you are moving a directory, the directory, all of its subdirectories, and all files are copied also.

If you are moving files to a different directory on the same disk drive, the place you are moving to can be a drive icon, directory icon, or directory window.

1. Be sure that the window you are moving from and the window that you are moving to are visible in the File Manager workspace.

   If you are moving files to a drive icon, the files go into the current directory in the drive icon.

2. If you are moving files to a different drive, press and hold down the Shift key. (Make sure that you have enough space on the floppy.)

3. Press and hold down the mouse button and drag the file to where you want it.

4. Let go of the mouse button when the file is where you want to move it.

   A confirmation dialog box appears asking whether you are sure that you want to move the file.

5. Click on the Yes command button or press the Enter key to move the file; click on the No command button if you don't want to move the file.

If the location where you are moving a file has a file with the same name, a dialog box appears asking whether you are sure you want to move the file, which will replace the existing file. The names, sizes, and time/date stamp are next to the files in the dialog box so that you can see whether you really want to overwrite the file.

Click on the Yes button if you want to overwrite the file or click on the No button to leave the file alone. If you are copying multiple files and you reach this dialog box and you are sure that you want to move the files, you can click on the Yes to All command button. The Yes to All command button allows you the luxury of not having to click on a Yes command button a zillion and a half times.

If you want to move more than one file:

1. Click on the first file that you want to move.
2. Press and hold down the Shift key.
3. Click on the last file that you want to move.

   When you click on the last file, all of the files between the first and the last files are highlighted.

   If you want more files in the highlighted list, hold down the Ctrl key as you select more individual files. By holding down the Ctrl key, you may also unselect from the highlighted list by clicking on files.

4. Click and hold down on the left mouse button on the bottom of the selection you have just made.
5. Drag the files to where you want them to go.
6. Let go of the mouse button and the Shift key.

Here's how to use the keyboard to move a file:

1. Press the F7 function key or press Alt, F, M. A dialog box appears.
2. In the From box, type in the filename that you want to move.
3. If the file that you want to move is not in the directory listed in the Current Directory portion of the dialog box, then type in the directory before the filename.
4. Press the Tab key to move to the To box.
5. Type in where you want the file to go, including the subdirectory and drive letter, if needed. Type in the filename.
6. Press the Tab key until you reach the OK command button. Press the Enter key to move the file; press the Esc key to exit and not move the files.

Moving the Split Bar

Used to change the view so that you can see more of the directory tree or more of the directory contents in the directory window.

To move the split bar, click on the split bar and hold down the left mouse button. Once you reach the split bar, the mouse's pointer icon turns to a two-headed icon with a bar in the middle. Move the bar to the left or right. When the split bar is where you want it, let go of the mouse button.

Steps

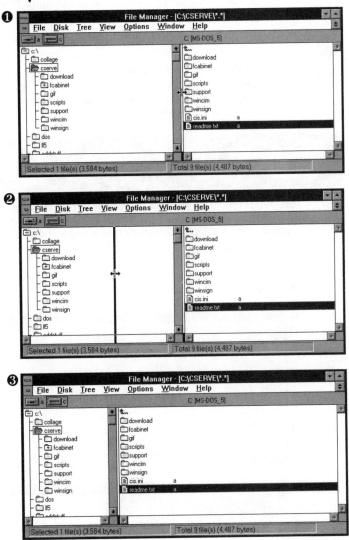

More stuff

You can also click on View, Split from the File Manager menu bar.

Moving the split bar only affects the active directory window.

If you want to save where you placed the split bar for future reference, click on Options, Save Settings on Exit from the File Manager menu bar. A check mark indicates that the command is on.

Here is the keyboard method of moving the split bar:

1. Press Alt, V, L.
2. Use the arrow keys to move the split bar to the left or right.
3. Press the Enter key to anchor the split bar in its new home, or press the Esc key to have Calgon take you away and not mess with the location of the split bar.

Opening More Than One Directory Window

Used to get multiple views of the same drive or view multiple drives. Opening more than one directory window is particularly helpful when you want to copy or move files and directories.

Double-click on a drive icon. Click on the Window, Tile command to see the open directory windows.

Steps

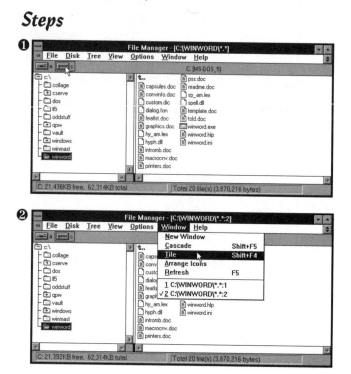

❸
[File Manager window screenshot]

File Manager

File   Disk   Tree   View   Options   Window   Help

C:\WINWORD*.*:2

C: [MS-DOS_5]
windows
winmast
winword

custom.dic   graphics.doc   intromb.doc   pss.d
capsules.doc   dialog.fon   hy_am.lex   macrocnv.doc   readn
convinfo.doc   featlst.doc   hyph.dll   printers.doc   sp_ar

C:\WINWORD*.*:1

C: [MS-DOS_5]
windows
winmast
winword

custom.dic   graphics.doc   intromb.doc   pss.d
capsules.doc   dialog.fon   hy_am.lex   macrocnv.doc   readn
convinfo.doc   featlst.doc   hyph.dll   printers.doc   sp_ar

C: 21,392KB free, 62,314KB total   Total 20 file(s) (3,870,216 bytes)

More stuff

To open a new directory window you can also

- Click on Window, New Window from the File Manager menu bar.

- Press and hold down the Shift key while double-clicking on a directory with the mouse.

- Select a directory and press Shift+Enter.

- Press Alt, W, N.

- Whew!

If you have two directory windows that are showing the same drive or directory, the windows' title bars show a number indicating that there is more than one copy open.

Just like in the Program Manager when you want to work within a window, you first have to make a window active. The same goes for a directory window in the File Manager. Click inside of a window to make the window active. You can make a window active by clicking on Window and then choosing the open window's name at the bottom of the Window pull-down menu. Another way to make a window active is to press Alt, W, and the number that corresponds to the window that you want to make active.

If there are too many windows to deal with or the windows are overlapping, click on Window, Cascade from the File Manager menu bar.

See "Arranging Directory Windows" earlier in this section to get the skinny on arranging spoiled windows.

If you have only one directory window open, you can't close it, so don't even try.

If you maximize a directory window, the title bar of the File Manager has the information that used to be in the title bar of the directory window before you maximized it.

See "Parts of a Directory Window" later in this section to figure out what a title bar is.

It may be to your advantage to stick with just one directory window open at any given time. Not only is it easier on your eyes, but it also keeps down the amount of memory Windows has to shell out to keep all of your directory windows open.

Parts of a Directory Window

Components used in the File Manager directory window so a user can accomplish actions within a window in a fashion similar to that of the Program Manager. Whew!

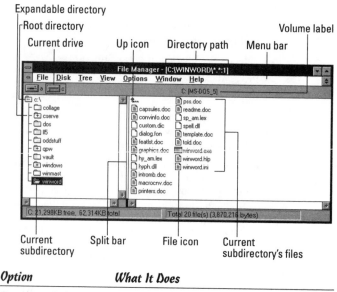

Expandable directory
Root directory
Current drive
Up icon
Directory path
Volume label
Menu bar

Current subdirectory
Split bar
File icon
Current subdirectory's files

Option	What It Does
Current subdirectory	Highlighted and represented by an open folder, this indicates the directory that you are using.
	In the right half of the directory window is the directory contents, which shows the names of directories and files within the current directory.

Option	What It Does
Directory path	Located in the title bar of the directory window (or the title bar of the File Manager if the window is maximized). The directory path lets you know where you are in the directory structure.
Root directory	Created when you format a disk. The root directory of the hard disk is usually C:\.
Split bar	Divides the directory window so that the directory tree is on the left and the directory contents are on the right. The split bar is only available if you have both the directory tree and the directory contents visible.
Up icon	Takes you up one directory level unless you're at the root directory where the up arrow disappears. Looks like a bent arrow with two dots beside it.
Volume label	The label of the current drive. If you're like me and never name your drives, this may just say "DOS".

Subdirectory and File Icons

What It Looks Like	What It Is / What It Does
📂	A subdirectory. The folder is *open,* so this subdirectory is currently spilling its contents onto the right side of the window so you can see all its files.
📁	A subdirectory. This folder is *closed,* so it's just sitting there. Double-click on it, and it opens, showing you what's inside.
▦	A file. This is a *program.* Double-click on this thing to bring the program to the screen.
📄	A file. This is a *data file.* Double-click here and the File Manager loads the file, along with the program that created it. Fast and automatic.
📄	A file. Windows can't figure out *what* this file is, so clicking on it just causes confusion. It's probably important, though, so don't delete it.

(continues)

What It Looks Like	What It Is / What It Does
⬜❗	A file. This is a hidden file. Windows tried to hide this file from you so you wouldn't mess with it. (So *don't* mess with it.)
🗀..	This isn't a file, but you'll see it anyway. If you click here, the File Manager shifts your view to the directory above the one you're currently looking at.

More stuff

You can maximize, minimize, move, or resize a directory window in the File Manager workspace. See "Parts of a Window" in Part I, "Windows Basics," for an explanation of all of these wonderful things.

Printing a File

Using the File Manager along with the Print Manager, you can print files that have an association with an application. Click and hold the mouse button on the document that you want to print. Drag the document icon to the minimized Print Manager icon. Let go of the mouse button. Alternatively, just choose File, Print from the File Manager menu bar.

Steps

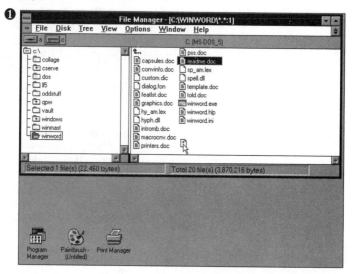

❷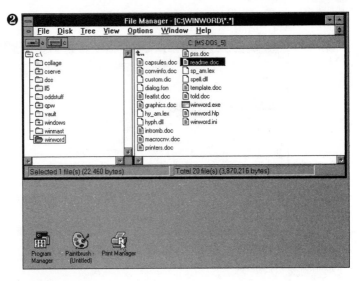

More stuff

Unfortunately, some applications do not support printing from the File Manager. To get around this problem, just print from within your application.

Make sure that the Print Manager is running and minimized as an icon on the desktop.

Renaming a File or Directory

Used to change the name of a file or directory.

Click on the file you want to rename. Click on File, Rename from the File Manager menu bar. The Rename dialog box appears on the screen. In the To box, type in the name that you want to change the file to. Click on the OK command button or press the Enter key to rename the file; press the Esc key to back out of renaming the file altogether.

Steps

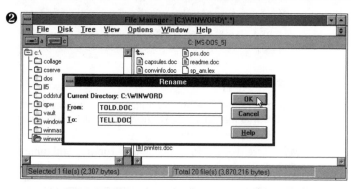

More stuff

You can rename a directory the same way that you rename a file; just click on the directory instead of a file in the example.

Another way to rename a file or directory is by putting the old name in the From section of the Rename dialog box and the new name in the To section.

You can also rename a group of files using a wild card — just like in poker. If you want to rename all of your TXT files so that they have DOC extensions, just put ***.TXT** in the From section of the Rename dialog box and ***.DOC** in the To section. Unless you've done this before, you may want to have a DOS or Windows guru show you the ropes.

Don't rename files that end in a SYS extension. Doing so makes your computer have a horrible time with your disk drive and may even cause you computer not to boot up. Other files that you shouldn't rename include those with the extensions EXE, COM, OVL, DLL, INI, and DRV. Also, don't rename program directories that were named through their installation.

Searching for a File or Directory

Used when you just can't seem to find the file you were working on last week.

Click on File, Search from the File Manager menu bar. The Search dialog box pops up on the screen. In the Search For box, type in the name that you want to search for. In the Start From box, tell Windows to begin searching at the root directory by putting in a \ (backslash) right after the drive letter and the colon (unless you know that the file is in a specific directory). Click on the OK command button or press the Enter key to start the search. The Search Results window shows up with the results of your search request. If you change your mind during the search, press the Esc key to stop the search for the file or directory.

Steps

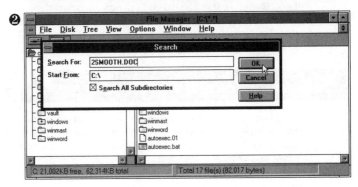

③

See the example in *Windows 3.1 For Dummies*, 2nd Edition, Chapter 12, "Finding the File You Saved Yesterday."

More stuff

Before you start a search, click on the root directory unless you know that the file is in a specific subdirectory. Doing this starts the search at the root directory and searches all of the directories and files on the current drive.

If you don't want to search all of the subdirectories on the current drive, in the Search dialog box, click on the Search All Sub-directories check box to deselect it.

If you know your way around wild cards, you can search for a group of files in the Search For box. Ask a DOS or Windows guru about wild cards if you really want to know about this arcane DOS stuff.

Every time you do a search, the Search Results window is cleared to make room for the new search.

If you want to cancel a search in progress, press the Esc key. The search stops, and the File Manager waits for you to do something else. The Search Results window appears, displaying all filenames and directories found up to that point.

Selecting Files and Directories

Used to work with a group of files or directories. If you want to work with more than one file or directory, you have to *extend* the selected file or directory to include the other files or directories. When you extend a selection, a bunch of files or directories become selected instead of just one.

Click on the file or directory that you want to start with and press and hold the Shift key. Click on the last file you want to include in the group. Let go of the Shift key. Now you can copy or move the whole lot. To deselect the current selection, click on a single file or directory without pressing the Shift key.

Steps

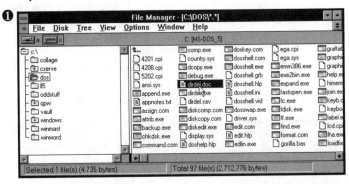

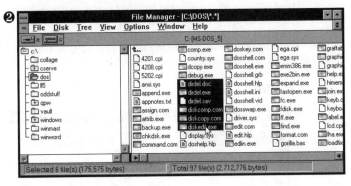

More stuff

You can also click on Files, Select Files from the File Manager menu bar. When the Select files dialog box appears, put the types of files that you want to select, using wild cards if necessary.

You can't load, print, or rename a group of files all at once. You have to do that one file at a time.

You can also use the following keys to select files next to each other:

1. Press the Tab key to move to the directory contents area.
2. Select the directory or file that you want to start with by using the up- or down-arrow keys.
3. Press and hold down the Shift key while using the arrow keys to extend to all of the files you want to select.
4. If you want all of the files in the directory contents area, hold down the Shift key and press the End or Home key.
5. Make a copy or move operation happen by pressing F7 or F8.

If you want to select files that aren't next to each other:

1. Press the Tab key to move to the directory contents area.
2. Select the directory or file that you want to start with by using the up- or down-arrow keys.
3. Press the Shift+F8 key combo.
4. Use the arrow keys to get to each individual file.
5. Press the spacebar to select or deselect individual files.
6. Make a copy or move operation happen by pressing F7 or F8.

Starting an Application with the File Manager

Used to start an application without using an application icon. Starting an application with the File Manager is especially handy if you want to start a non-Windows application. Find a file in the directory contents side of the directory window with a BAT, COM, EXE, or PIF filename extension. Double-click on the file.

Steps

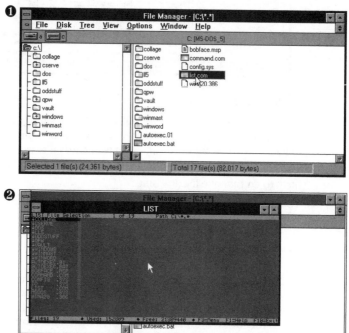

More stuff

You can shrink the File Manager to an icon every time you start
an application by clicking on the Options, Minimize on Use
command from the menu bar. A check mark next to the command
means it's on.

If you know the filename and its extension and location, you can
use the File, Run command from the menu bar. Click on the OK
command button to start the application or press the Esc key to
abort the whole kit-and-caboodle. The Run Minimized check box
in this dialog box, when selected, allows the application to start
as an icon.

To use the keyboard to start an application with File Manager:

1. Press Tab to get to the directory contents side of the
   directory window.
2. Use the arrow keys to get to the file with the appropriate
   extension.
3. Press the Enter key to let the fun begin.

Starting File Manager

Used to get the File Manager up and running.

Double-click on the Main group icon in the Program Manager.
Then double-click on the File Manager icon.

Steps

❶
Program Manager

File   Options   Window   Help

CompuServe

Accessories   Games   LapLink V   StartUp   Applications   Document   Main
                                                           Window

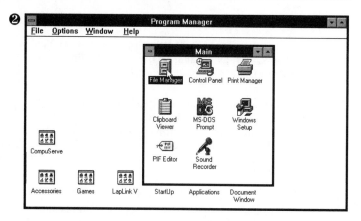

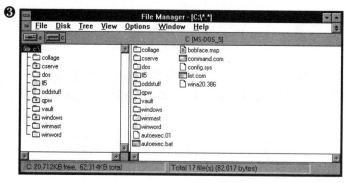

More stuff

If you've ever worked with the DOS shell in DOS 5 or later, this looks very much like it, and you'll feel very much at home.

You may say to yourself, "Hey, that looks just like the Program Manager." Don't fool yourself. The File Manager and Program Manager may have many similarities, but the biggest difference is that the Program Manager's icons are just buttons that stand for your applications. The names and icons in the File Manager are the actual programs and subdirectories. In the Program Manager, you're shooting blanks; in the File Manager you've got real bullets, and you can easily blow away a file. Permanently.

Part V:
Control Panel

386 Enhanced

Tells Windows how to control simultaneous requests from applications for external devices such as printers and modems.

This item is also used for telling Windows which application should get priority over another when Windows is running both Windows and non-Windows applications. Double-click on this icon in the Control Panel.

Steps

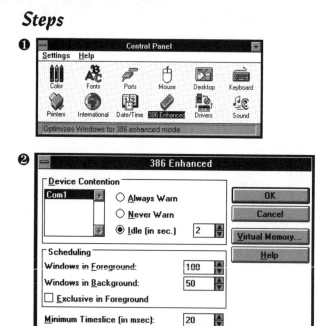

See the example in *Windows 3.1 For Dummies,* 2nd Edition, Chapter 10, "Examining Scary 386 Enhanced and Swap Files Stuff," and the example in *MORE Windows For Dummies*, Chapter 11, "Swap Files (That Virtual Memory Stuff)."

Read this only as a primer for a good nap.

Dialog Box Options	*What You Can Do with Them*
Device Contention: Ports	Just a fancy way of having Windows ask you what you want it to do in case two ports — the places where data is sent out of the computer — crash head on into one another.

Dialog Box Options	*What You Can Do with Them*
	Click on one of the port names listed in this box and click on the radio button Idle. This option should have a setting of two seconds. If you're curious about what Never Warn means, don't be; it just means that you can have corrupt data being pumped out one of your data ports and Windows won't tell you.
Minimum Timeslice	Lets Windows know how much of its time it should give to each running application.
	Leave this number set at the default. Windows knows how to handle its time so that things run smoothly, and it can take care of this number automatically.
System in Foreground	Click on this check box if you want Windows to be snooty and give Windows applications 100 percent attention when a Windows application is running and ignore non-Windows applications.
Virtual Memory	Click on this button to change things like swap file size and type. Ever heard of Pandora? This one is best left to a Windows guru.
Windows in Background	Tells Windows how much time it should give to Windows applications when a non-Windows application is running. This number is usually 100 but can range from 1 to 10,000. Just leave this option alone.
Windows in Foreground	Tells Windows how much time it should give to the active application when multiple applications are crying for Windows' attention. This number is usually 100 but can range from 1 to 10,000. Just leave this option alone.

More stuff

Here's the keyboard shortcut from the Control Panel window: Alt, S, 3.

Changing the Desktop Color Scheme

Changes the color scheme of an application window, including the title bar, border, scroll bar, and text window colors. Double-click on the Color icon in the Control Panel.

Steps

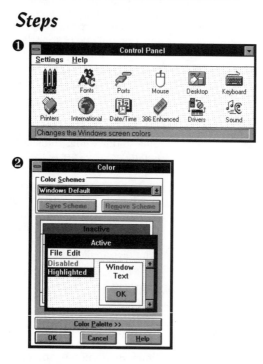

Dialog Box Options	*What You Can Do with Them*
Color Schemes	Drop-down list box that allows you to select one of a variety of different predefined color schemes that Windows has to offer.
	Each name in the list box changes the colors of several screen elements at once. If you're really into colors, you can modify the current color scheme or make new color schemes by saving your changes with a new name. When you make changes, you can see your selection in the preview area.

Dialog Box Options	*What You Can Do with Them*
	The Save Scheme command button allows you to save your new color-coordinated settings. The Remove Scheme button (which is not recommended for general use because you can delete a perfectly good scheme) allows you to remove a color scheme. Press the Esc key if you've made a mistake or the Cancel command button at the bottom of the dialog box to undo any changes you may have made.
Color Palette	Command button that gives you two palettes where you can choose colors for individual screen elements.
	Your changes are shown in the preview area. A lot of time can be spent playing around with different types of color schemes for your desktop. If you've always wanted to be an interior designer, you can hone your skills here.

More stuff

Here's the keyboard shortcut from the Control Panel window: Alt, S, C.

Changing Desktop Options

Changes desktop options like background pattern or wallpaper, screen savers, the cursor blink rate, how far the icons are from one another, grid size, and window border width. Double-click on this icon in the Control Panel.

Steps

❷

Desktop
Pattern
N<u>a</u>me: [None]
Edit <u>P</u>attern...
OK
Cancel
<u>H</u>elp
Applications
☒ Fast "Al<u>t</u>+Tab" Switching
Screen Saver
N<u>a</u>me: [None]
<u>D</u>elay: 2 Minutes
Test
Setup...
Wallpaper
<u>F</u>ile: [None]
○ <u>C</u>enter ◉ <u>T</u>ile
Icons
Spacing: 75 Pixels
☒ <u>W</u>rap Title
Sizing Grid
<u>G</u>ranularity: 0
<u>B</u>order Width: 3
Cursor Blink <u>R</u>ate
Slow Fast

See the example in *Windows 3.1 For Dummies,* 2nd Edition, Chapter 10, "Customizing the Desktop," and the example in *MORE Windows For Dummies*, Chapter 10, "Desktops on Other People's Computers."

You'll probably find yourself wandering in here to play with Windows' miscellaneous options.

Dialog Box Options	*What You Can Do with Them*
Pattern	Drop-down list box that allows you to select one of a variety of different patterns for your desktop background.
	Use the scroll bars or the up- and down-arrow keys to look at all the options. Double-click on a name that you want to select for the desktop background. The Edit Pattern dialog box allows you to get creative in making and naming your own desktop background. *Hint:* Don't use the remove button unless you really have to.
Applications	Use this check box. Period. This feature is one of the better ones in Windows.
	Having this check box selected gives you a small box with an application name in it every time you press and hold down the Alt key and press Tab. Pressing Tab repeatedly while holding down the Alt key displays the name of the application Windows will switch to. When you find the application you want to use, let go of the Alt key to switch to that application.
Screen Saver	Drop-down list box that allows you to select one of a variety of different screen

Dialog Box Options	*What You Can Do with Them*
	savers that are displayed when you are not actively using Windows.
	You can use the screen savers that come with Windows, or you can use the screen savers that come with the Microsoft Entertainment Pack — if you were lucky enough to get it. There are four options in this box:
	• Name gives you the five different screen savers you can choose from, including a blank screen and a starfield simulation.
	• Delay gives you the choice of how many minutes of inactivity — not touching the keyboard or the mouse — must pass before the screen saver jumps into action.
	• Test lets you see what the screen saver looks like when it pops up; press any key on the keyboard to get out of the test.
	• Setup lets you change options for each screen saver. If you select the Marquee setup, for example, you can write your own message that will scroll across the screen when the screen saver pops up. Also use Setup to set a password for the system when the screen saver is running.
Wallpaper	Drop-down list box that allows you to select one of a variety of different desktop backgrounds with a bitmap (BMP) file.
	You can use bitmaps that were made in Paintbrush or in any drawing or painting application that saves files with a BMP extension in the Windows directory. Only use this option if you have lots of memory in your system, because this option can slow down your computer, especially if you select the Tile radio button.
Icons	Allows you to select how far apart the icons are from each other and whether the title of the icon wraps underneath the first line of the title.
	The check box should be checked, and the spacing should be left at the default.
Sizing Grid	Sizes the individual windows' borders and sets the invisible spacing that Windows

(continues)

Dialog Box Options	What You Can Do with Them
	uses to line up windows and icons on the desktop. It's best to leave these options at the default.
Cursor Blink Rate	Determines how fast the text cursor blinks in word processing applications.
	To increase or decrease the cursor blink rate, use the mouse to drag the scroll bar. There is a cursor to the right of the scroll bar, so you can see what your changes do. Unless you really have a problem with how fast the cursor blinks, leave this option at the default.

More stuff

Here's the keyboard shortcut from the Control Panel window: Alt, S, D.

Configuring a Communication Port

Changes the baud rate, parity, data bit, stop bits, and flow control of your serial or COM ports. Chances are that this stuff is already configured correctly. Double-click on the Ports icon in the Control Panel.

Steps

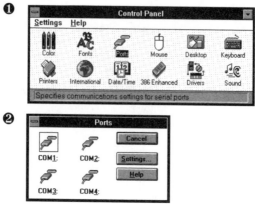

More stuff

Ask a Windows guru about this stuff.

Here's the keyboard shortcut from the Control Panel window:
Alt, S, O.

Date and Time

Sets the date and time. Double-click on the Date/Time icon in the
Control Panel.

To change the day, highlight the day by clicking and holding the
left mouse button while dragging across the date. Use the up- and
down-arrow keys to change the date or change the date with the
number keys on the keyboard. Click on the OK button or press
Enter to save your changes or press Esc to exit without making
any changes.

Steps

❶

❷

More stuff

Here's the keyboard shortcut from the Control Panel window:
Alt, S, T.

Drivers

Installs a sound card, video player card, or MIDI device to
Windows after you have actually installed the physical card in the
computer.

Windows doesn't recognize the card unless you have configured
the driver for that card. You can install a driver, select a driver,
remove a driver, or change a driver's settings. Double-click on the
Drivers icon in the Control Panel.

Steps

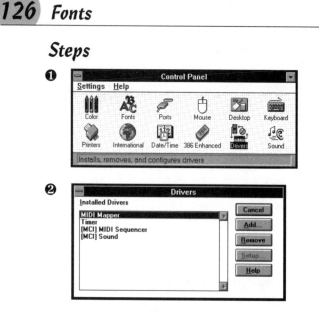

❶

❷

 See the example in *Windows 3.1 For Dummies,* 2nd Edition, Chapter 17, "I'm Supposed to Install a New 'Driver,'" and the example in *MORE Windows For Dummies*, Chapter 3, "How to install drivers."

More stuff

Ask a Windows guru about this stuff. Here's the keyboard shortcut from the Control Panel window: Alt, S, R.

Fonts

Adds or removes fonts from Windows. A new font technology, called TrueType, was introduced with Windows 3.1.

This new technology does away with jagged fonts — both on the screen and on the printer — and allows what you see on the screen to match what comes out of the printer. Double-click on the Fonts icon in the Control Panel.

Steps

❶

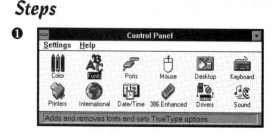

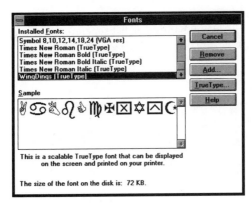

 See the example in *Windows 3.1 For Dummies,* 2nd Edition, Chapter 10, "Understanding the Fuss about TrueType Fonts," and the example in *MORE Windows For Dummies*, Chapter 3, "A Font of Font Wisdom."

More stuff

You will probably never need to fiddle with the Fonts icon.

If you want to install more fonts, this is the place to do it.

 Here's the keyboard shortcut from the Control Panel window: Alt, S, F.

Fonts can take up quite a bit of hard disk space. If you have installed additional fonts to Windows and you don't use them anymore, delete them:

1. Click on the name of the font you no longer use.

2. Click on the Remove option button. A dialog box appears, asking whether you are sure that you want to remove the font.

3. Before clicking on the Yes button, click on the check-marked box Delete Font File From Disk; otherwise, Windows removes that font only from the Font menus, and the font files still clog up the hard drive.

   But, if you have enough room for these extra fonts, don't delete them from the hard drive. It's harder to install fonts than to delete them. Other applications use special fonts in their display, so be very careful when deleting fonts.

International Settings

Used for international applications that use these settings.

This item is for changing things like country, keyboard layout, currency and number format, list separator, language, date and time format, and measurement. Double-click on the International icon in the Control Panel.

Steps

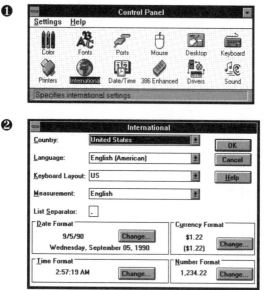

Dialog Box Options	What You Can Do with Them
Country	Drop-down list box that allows you to change to any of the countries supported by Windows.
Currency Format	Change command button that allows you to change your currency formats to standard accounting or other formats.
Date Format	Change command button that allows you to change different options for different international settings and the order that dates are presented.
Keyboard Layout	Drop-down list box that allows you to change to a different country's keyboard layout.
	You can also use this option to change to a Dvorak keyboard layout; ask a Windows guru if you've never heard of this layout and are curious about it.

Dialog Box Options	*What You Can Do with Them*
Language	Drop-down list box that allows you to select a different language for Windows, such as English, French, German, or Spanish. This might be a good place to start augmenting those language learning tapes you have in your closet.
List Separator	Your list separator is usually a comma. Leave this setting at the default.
Measurement	Drop-down list box that allows you to select between an English or a Metric measurement.
Number Format	Change command button that allows you to change the thousands separator, the decimal separator, and whether numbers have leading zeros.
Time Format	Change command button that allows you to change time formats for different time settings, such as 12- or 24-hour formats.

More stuff

Get out your Windows disks if you plan to play here.

Here's the keyboard shortcut from the Control Panel window: Alt, S, F.

Mouse

Used for changing the double-click speed of the mouse, setting the mouse tracking speed, and changing the mouse buttons for a left-handed person. Double-click on the Mouse icon in the Control Panel.

Steps

❶

Control Panel

Settings   Help

Color   Fonts   Ports   Mouse   Desktop   Keyboard

Printers   International   Date/Time   386 Enhanced   Drivers   Sound

Changes settings for your mouse

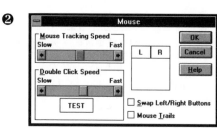

Dialog Box Options	*What You Can Do with Them*
Double Click Speed	Scroll bar that allows you to change the speed at which Windows recognizes a double-click.
	Use the Test box to see what double-click speed is best for you. (If you're having trouble double-clicking on icons to open them, this setting fixes the problem.)
Mouse Tracking Speed	Scroll bars let you change the speed at which Windows allows the mouse pointer to travel across the screen. This option is worth playing with for better mouse control.
Mouse Trails	Check box that improves the visibility of the mouse pointer by stretching the mouse out whenever you move the mouse — also known as ghosting. Creepy, huh?
	This option is recommended if you are using a notebook computer that has an LCD display. This option is dimmed if your display driver does not support mouse trails.
Swap Left/Right Buttons	If you're left-handed, this option may be more comfortable.

More stuff

This is a great place to play around with learning how to use the mouse.

Here's the keyboard shortcut from the Control Panel window: Alt, S, M.

Printers

Installs and removes printers, changes printer settings, and selects the printer to use as the default printer.

Double-click on the Printers icon in the Control Panel.

Steps

❶

Control Panel window showing Settings and Help menus with icons: Color, Fonts, Ports, Mouse, Desktop, Keyboard, Printers, International, Date/Time, 386 Enhanced, Drivers, Sound. Status bar: "Installs and removes printers, and sets printing options."

❷
Printers dialog box:
Default Printer
HP LaserJet Series II on LPT1:
Installed Printers:
HP LaserJet IIP on LPT1:
HP LaserJet Series II on LPT1:
Set As Default Printer
☒ Use Print Manager
Buttons: Cancel, Connect..., Setup..., Remove, Add >>, Help

See the example in *Windows 3.1 For Dummies,* 2nd Edition, Chapter 10, "Adding or Removing a Printer."

Dialog Box Options	What You Can Do with Them
Add	Click on the Add button to install a printer.
	Choosing this button displays a List of Printers section. List of Printers shows most of the printers supported by Windows.
Connect	Clicking on the Connect command button displays the Connect dialog box.
	When here, you can assign a printer to a port, specify a timeout option, or select the Fast Printing to Port check box. This stuff is best left at the default unless you want to change a port, in which case you'd better get the six pack of Twinkies for the Windows guru.
Default Printer	Shows you what printer is selected as the default printer.

(continues)

Dialog Box Options	What You Can Do with Them
	The *default printer* is the printer that all applications send documents to when you select Print from within an application.
Installed Printers	Displays a list of the installed printers.
Remove	Click on the Remove button to remove the highlighted printer from the installed printers list.
	If you use the Remove button, the driver file is still left on the hard disk (as are the font files) because another printer may be using the same driver or fonts or both. So why use it? To quench that destructive urge.
Set As Default Printer	Click on this command button after you have selected a different printer in the Installed Printers area than shown in the Default Printer area. The newly selected printer becomes the one that all printouts will go to.
Setup	Clicking on the Setup command button displays the dialog box for setting printer options.
	The only major options here that you want to mess with are choosing whether to print in Portrait or Landscape and selecting how many copies of everything you want to print. All the options in this dialog box may vary depending on which printer you have selected.
Use Print Manager	Click on the Use Print Manager check box if you want to turn on the Print Manager.
	When the Print Manager is on, you can print several documents at a time and not have to wait for the application you are printing from to return from printing.
	If the Print Manager check box is not checked, documents may print faster, but you will have to wait for the printer to finish printing a document before you can send another document to the printer or go back to working in your application.

More stuff

Get out your Windows disks if you plan to do any messing with printers.

If your boss wants you to print the Ferguson report to the fancy-schmancy laserjet instead of printing to the usual old line printer, here's how to do it:

1. Double-click on the printer in the Installed Printers list box that you want to use as the new default printer.

2. Click on the Set As Default Printer command button.

3. Click on the Close command button.

To add a new printer, follow these steps:

1. Click on the Add button. A list of printers magically appears. Use the scroll bar to search for the printer that you want to install (you can also use the up or down arrow or the Page Up and Page Down keys to scroll through the list of printers).

2. Click on the printer's name that you want to select.

3. Click on the Install command button. Windows will ask you to insert one of the setup disks. After a bit of crunching on the disk, you'll see the new printer listed.

4. Click on the Set As Default Printer command button.

5. Click on the Close command button.

Here's the keyboard shortcut from the Control Panel window: Alt, S, P.

Sound

Gives sounds to Windows systems' events.

This command only works if you have a sound card or a file called a wave driver for sound files with the extension WAV in your system. If you don't have a sound card installed, the list of sounds and events appears dimmed. Double-click on the Sound icon in the Control Panel.

Steps

❶

Control Panel
Settings   Help
Color   Fonts   Ports   Mouse   Desktop   Keyboard
Printers   International   Date/Time   386 Enhanced   Drivers   Sound
Assigns sounds to system events

❷

Sound		
Events:	Files:	
Asterisk	<none>	**OK**
Critical Stop	bobspk.wav	**Cancel**
Default Beep	chimes.wav	
Exclamation	chord.wav	**Test**
Question	ding.wav	
Windows Exit	tada.wav	**Help**
Windows Start	[...]	
	[msapps]	
☒ E**n**able System Sounds	c:\windows	

See the example in *Windows 3.1 For Dummies,* 2nd Edition, Chapter 2, "Sound Cards (Making Barfing Noises)" and "Fun CD-ROM Stuff." Also see Chapter 10, "Making Cool Barf Sounds with Multimedia," and the example in *MORE Windows For Dummies,* Chapter 3, "Adding or Changing Sounds."

Dialog Box Options	*What You Can Do with Them*
Enable System Sounds	You can turn on or off the Windows warning beep that Windows uses to indicate an error if you do not have a sound card by clicking on the Enable System Sounds check box.
	This check box does not disable Windows start and exit sounds unless you have a sound card and select <none> for the Windows start and exit events.
Events	Click on the event that you want to assign a particular sound to and then click on the sound file in the Files box. If you don't want to assign a sound, click on <none>.
Test	This command button lets you hear what the selected file in the Files box sounds like. A great place to listen to such classics as Ta-Da and Bronx Cheer.

More stuff

Here's the keyboard shortcut from the Control Panel window: Alt, S, S.

Starting the Control Panel

Gets at all of the nifty functions in this section.

Double-click on the Main group icon. Double-click on the Control Panel icon.

Steps

❶
```
                         Program Manager
 File   Options   Window   Help




 Accessories   Games   LapLink V   StartUp   Applications   Document   Main
                                                            Window
```

❷
```
                    Main
 File Manager   Control Panel   Print Manager

 Clipboard   MS-DOS   Windows
 Viewer      Prompt   Setup

 PIF Editor   Sound
              Recorder
```

❸
```
                   Control Panel
 Settings   Help

 Color   Fonts   Ports   Mouse   Desktop   Keyboard

 Printers   International   Date/Time   386 Enhanced   Drivers   Sound

 Optimizes Windows for 386 enhanced mode.
```

What the Icon Says	What the Switch Does
Color	Windows installs boring colors at first. You use the Color icon to liven things up by changing the colors of the bars, buttons, background, and everything else. Fun!
Fonts	Windows comes with fonts like Arial and Courier. If you head back to the software store and buy more, like Lucida Blackletter and Lucida Handwriting, you install them by double-clicking on this icon.

(continues)

What the Icon Says	What the Switch Does
Ports	If you have a *modem* or a *serial printer* plugged into the computer's rump, they're actually plugged into *ports*. This icon changes those port settings. (If your stuff already works, don't ever click here.)
Mouse	Make that mouse scoot faster across the screen, change it from right-handed to left-handed, and change all sorts of other things.
Desktop	This one provides a plethora of options to while away the day. Change the wallpaper, screen saver, and other fun stuff.
Keyboard	You can change how long the keyboard takes to repeat a letter when you hold down a key. Yawn. Rarely used.
Printers	Bought a new printer? You have to fiddle around in here to let Windows know about the printer.
International	Packed up the computer and moved to Sweden? Then click around in here to get those funny foreign characters.
Date/Time	Does the Windows clock tell the right time? If not, double-click here to bring things up to date.
Network	Yech. Let your network folks mess with this one. They're getting paid extra for it.
386 Enhanced	Like race-car mechanics, computer gurus with 386 computers can fiddle around in here for hours. Don't play in here unless a nearby computer guru can serve as Safety Patrol. This is scary stuff.
Drivers	Opened your wallet for a sound card? Then open this icon to install its driver. It tells Windows what brand of sound card you decided on.
MIDI Mapper	It's used mostly by musicians with synthesizers. And it's ugly, technical stuff. Toss in a Lou Reed CD for an attitude boost before entering the grim world of Source Channels and Patch Names.
Sound	The most fun! Make Windows play different sounds for different events. For example, hear a cool Pink Floyd riff whenever a Windows error message pops up on the screen.

Part VI:

Windows for Workgroups

Installing Windows for Workgroups

You can think of Windows for Workgroups as regular old Windows 3.1 (or 3.11) with a twist — the twist being its support for a bunch of *networking* stuff. (For a really good explanation of the differences between regular Windows and Windows for Workgroups, see "How Does Windows Differ from Windows for Workgroups?" in *Windows 3.1 For Dummies*, 2nd Edition). This special version of Windows was developed for offices where certain groups of personal computers are tied together on a *local area network* (LAN). Windows for Workgroups facilitates stuff like sharing files stored on the hard disk of a remote computer, using someone else's printer, and, of course, exchanging messages with your office mates.

TIP

You can run Windows for Workgroups on your computer even if you're not tied into a network. It runs just like regular old Windows, except that it runs everything a whole bunch faster.

Installing Windows for Workgroups is just like installing Windows, meaning that you don't ever want to try it yourself. Instead, cajole whoever has the unenviable responsibility of maintaining the network to do it for you. This is especially true if you want to upgrade a computer from regular Windows 3.1 or 3.11 to Windows for Workgroups using Express Setup — you may not be able to complete the installation (meaning that you can no longer run Windows 3.11 or any of your Windows programs) if the setup program doesn't automatically recognize the particular type of network you're using.

CROSS REFERENCE

See the example in *Windows 3.1 For Dummies*, 2nd Edition, Chapter 3, "Installing Windows for Workgroups."

Logging On and Off the Network

Assuming that you've conned your network administrator (or a facsimile thereof) to install and set up Windows for Workgroups for you, you are ready to — in the parlance of a true networker — *log on*. To log on, you type **WIN** and press Enter just as if you were starting good old Windows 3.1. However, when you start Windows for Workgroups, the program displays the Welcome to Windows dialog box, displaying the pet name you have for your computer (such as LOSER) in the Logon Name edit box. If you share the computer with other people (poor baby!), each person can have his or her pet name for the computer, which he or she enters into the Logon Name edit box when logging on to Windows for Workgroups.

If your network administrator has assigned you a password, you must accurately type it into the Password box of the Welcome to Windows for Workgroups dialog box. If you don't use passwords in your office, just leave this dialog box alone and choose the OK button or press Enter.

Steps

❶
| Welcome to Windows for Workgroups |
Type a logon name and password to log on to the Microsoft Windows Network.

MICROSOFT. WINDOWS.

Logon Name: `GREG`

Password: [   ]

OK **Cancel** **Help**

When you get tired of sharing other people's messages, files, and printers, you can log off the network by double-clicking on the Log On/Off icon in the Network group window. After you log off, you no longer have access to any of the resources on the network (like Sheila's color laser printer and Fred's personnel evaluation files). However, everybody else can still use your printer and steal your files blind. To get back on the network (where all the action is) while you're still in Windows, just double-click on the Log On/Off icon again.

 See the example in *Windows 3.1 For Dummies*, 2nd Edition, Chapter 20, "Just Tell Me How to 'Log On' and 'Log Off' a Network!"

Sharing Files

The big deal about networks is that you can use other people's files without getting involved with all that copying to floppy disk stuff. Before you can get access to somebody else's files (or somebody else can steal yours), the directory containing the goodies must be set up as a *shared directory*.

To make a directory a shared directory or to get connected to somebody else's shared directory, you need to open the File Manager (see Part IV, "File Manager," if you need help with this). The File Manager in Windows for Workgroups contains a new toolbar wedged between the pull-down menus and the drive bar. The toolbar offers a group of buttons designed to facilitate file sharing.

```
File Manager - [C:\VB\*.* - [MS-DOS_6]]
File   Disk   Tree   View   Options   Tools   Window   Help
C: [MS-DOS_6]
a    b    c    d    h
```

```
              Connect        Share   Stop
              Network        As      Sharing
              Drive
                             Disconnect
                             Network
                             Drive
```

Sharing Your Directories

To share one of your precious directories on the hard disk with
all your workgroup pals, follow these steps:

1. Open the File Manager. In the directory window, select the
    directory you want to share.

2. Click on the Share As button on the toolbar or choose Share
    As on the Disk pull-down menu to open the Shared Direc-
    tory dialog box.

3. Type in the name you want to give your shared directory or
    accept the name that appears in the Share Name edit box.

4. If you want to annotate the name of the shared directory as
    it appears in the Connect Network dialog box, type in your
    note in the Comment edit box.

5. If you don't want it to be open season on this directory
    each time you start Windows for Workgroups, deselect the
    Re-share at Startup check box.

6. Select the type of access you want to grant to your fellow
    workgroupers: Read-Only (they can look at and copy but
    not change your files); Full (they can do anything they want,
    including renaming, copying, or even getting rid of your
    babies); or Depends on Password (they can do anything
    they want provided that they know the password you
    assign).

7. Type a read-only password or general password in the
    Passwords edit boxes if you want to password-protect the
    shared directory.

8. Choose the OK button or press Enter.

Steps

❶

```
                                File Manager
 File   Disk   Tree   View   Options   Tools   Window   Help
 ▣ C: [MS-DOS_6]
 ▭ ▭

                           Share Directory
 ▭ ▭                                                        C:\BETH\*.* - [MS-DOS_6]
        Share Name:  BETH              [  OK  ]            ⬆ 🔼 ..
 📁 c:\                                                         📄 xlm01fi.doc
   📁 beth   Path:      C:\BETH          [ Cancel ]             📄 pkunzip.exe
   📁 bin                                                       📄 xlm01fi.zip
   📁 books  Comment:                   [  Help  ]
   📁 colldos
   📂 collwin             ☒ Re-share at Startup
   📁 compnev ┌─Access Type:─────────────────┐
   📁 compold │  ◉ Read-Only                 │
   📁 cserve  │  ○ Full                      │
   📁 data    │  ○ Depends on Password       │
   📁 dev     └──────────────────────────────┘
   📁 dos     ┌─Passwords:───────────────────┐
   📁 gwswin  │ Read-Only Password: [      ] │
   📁 iti     │ Full Access Password: [    ] │
   📁 mouse   └──────────────────────────────┘
   📁 msoffice            📄 install.log         📁 msoffice
   📁 olg                 📄 screen00.pcx        📁 olg
   📁 orgplus             📄 original.set        📁 orgplus
   📁 pcw_wp6             📄 readme.txt          📁 pcw_wp6
   📁 pkware                                     📁 pkware
   📁 qtemp                                      📁 qtemp
   📁 se                                         📁 se
   📁 sspro                                      📁 sspro

 Selected 0 file(s) (0 bytes)   Total 3 file(s) (128KB)
```

When you've had enough of your coworkers trashing the files in your shared directory, click on the Stop Sharing button on the File Manager toolbar (or choose Stop Sharing on the Disk pull-down menu). Then double-click on the name of the directory you no longer want to use (or select it and choose OK).

If other people are using the directory that you are trying to stop sharing, Windows displays an alert box prompting you for confirmation to dump them. If you go ahead and cold-bloodedly choose the Yes button, you may well cause them to lose their data (not that it wouldn't serve some of them right, because it's your data they're messing with!).

See the example in *Windows 3.1 For Dummies*, 2nd Edition, Chapter 20, "Sharing hard disk directories."

Using Somebody Else's Shared Directory

To get stuff from somebody else's shared directory, you need to connect to that directory as follows:

1. Click on the Connect Network Drive button on the File Manager toolbar (or choose Connect Network Drive on the Disk pull-down menu) to open the Connect Network Drive dialog box.

2. Select the letter of the drive containing the shared directory in the Drive drop-down list box.

3. Select the name of the computer containing the directory you want to connect to in the Show Shared Directories list box.

4. Select the name of the directory you want to access in the Shared Directories list box. (The list box name will be followed by the name of the computer you selected in Step 3.)

5. Choose the OK button or press Enter.

After you're connected, you can then use the files in this directory as though they were your very own (unless, of course, the shared directory has been assigned *read-only* status).

Steps

❶

When you've wreaked enough havoc on your coworker's files in the shared directory, click on the Disconnect Network Drive button on the File Manager toolbar (or choose Disconnect Network Drive on the Disk pull-down menu). Then double-click on the name of the directory you no longer want to use (or select it and choose OK).

Sharing Your Printer

If you want to share your printer with everyone in the group (aren't you sweet), you need to go through the same rigmarole as you do when sharing your directories. (Read the "Sharing Files" sections earlier for a refresher.) Only this time, you use the Print Manager:

1. Open the Print Manager.

2. Choose the name of your printer in the Print Manager window.

3. Choose Share Printer As on the Printer pull-down menu to open the Share Printer dialog box.

4. If you feel compelled, type in the name you want to give your shared printer (like *Greg's One and Only Laser Printer*) in the Share as edit box; add a comment to appear next to the printer name in the Print Manager window in the Comment edit box; and/or password-protect the printer by entering a password in the Password edit box.

5. Unless you're forced to share the printer all the time (or you're just a natural philanthropist), deselect the Re-share at Startup check box.

6. Choose OK or press Enter.

After you make your printer a shared printer, anyone can use it by opening the Print Manager, choosing the Connect Network Printer command on the Printer menu, and then selecting its name in the Printer Manager's list box and pressing Enter.

When you're tired of picking up other people's print jobs off your printer, you can disconnect it from the network (and then keep it all to yourself) by opening the Print Manager, choosing the Stop Sharing Printer command on the Printer menu, selecting the printer, and pressing Enter.

See the example in *Windows 3.1 For Dummies*, 2nd Edition, Chapter 20, "Sharing printers."

Using Mail

As if you hadn't had enough of this sharing stuff, Windows for Workgroups also lets you freely share your thoughts with coworkers in your workgroup using its electronic Mail program (just watch out for "flame" mail from some flounder!). Before you can use the Mail program, you have to bribe the network administrator into giving you the name of the computer and the location of the shared directory that contains the "post office" (where electronic mail is delivered) and set up your account (with your name, the name of your mailbox, and, if security warrants, a password that you enter to sign on to the Mail program).

Windows for Workgroups also includes a cute little application called Chat that you can use to send messages back and forth between your workgroup buddies. For information on using this applet, see the example in *Windows 3.1 For Dummies*, 2nd Edition, Chapter 20, "Chatting to someone else."

Entering the Mail System

To sign onto the Mail system and either send or receive mail (after you have an account set up and know where the post office is), you do this:

1. Double-click on the Mail icon in the Network group in the Program Manager.

2. Enter your Mail ID number in the Mailbox text box in the Mail Sign In dialog box. If you need to supply a password, type it in the Password text box in the Mail Sign In dialog box.

3. Choose OK or press Enter.

To quit Mail but remain signed in at the post office, you choose Exit on Mail's File pull-down menu. If new mail arrives, your computer will beep. If you want to disconnect from Mail completely, choose Exit and Sign Out on the File menu. People will still be able to send messages to your mailbox, but your computer won't beep when the messages arrive.

Getting Your Messages

After you're inside the electronic post office, your messages are listed in the Inbox dialog box, showing the name of the sender, the subject of the message, and the date received (you can always tell when a message is new because it's preceded by an icon showing a closed envelope). To read one of your messages in the Inbox dialog box, double-click on the message, which opens the text of the message in its own dialog box.

Replying to Messages

To reply to a message that you've displayed, click on the Reply button on the Mail toolbar (or choose Reply on the Mail pull-down menu). The Mail program opens an RE (Regarding) dialog box with the name of your message, automatically addresses your reply message to the sender, and positions the insertion point at the beginning of a blank line right above the text of the message that you received.

When you finish typing the text of your reply message, select the Send button at the top of the window to ship your reply off to the sender.

If the To and/or Cc: (carbon copy) edit boxes are filled in with the names of the other workgroup buddies who all received the message you're replying to, you can send copies of your reply message to everyone by choosing the Reply All button (rather than Reply) on the Mail toolbar.

Sending Messages

If you want to compose a new message instead of just replying to the mail that you get from your fellow workgroupers, click on the Compose button on the Mail toolbar (or choose Compose Note on the Mail pull-down menu). Then fill in the recipient's name in the To edit box (if you want to send the same message to a bunch of different people in the group, separate their names with a semicolon, as in **Corbin Collins; Diane Steele; Mary Bednarek**). Type the subject of your message in the Subject edit box. If you want other people in the group to be copied on the message, enter their names, again separated by semicolons, in the Cc: edit box. Type the text of your message in the message area and then click on the Send button to shuffle the message off to Buffalo.

Part VII:

Keystroke Shortcuts in Windows

Keystroke Shortcuts in Windows

General Keystrokes	Results
F1	Calls up the help menu
Alt+Enter	Toggles a DOS application from a window to full screen in 386 Enhanced mode
Alt+F+A	Saves a file under a new name in an application
Alt+F+N	Starts a new file in an application
Alt+F+O	Opens an existing file in an application
Alt+F+P	Prints a file in an application
Alt+F+S	Saves a file in an application
Alt+spacebar, N	Minimizes an application to an icon
Alt+spacebar, X	Maximizes an application so that it fills the screen
Alt+Tab+Tab	Moves from one application to another
Alt+F4	Closes a window, application, or Windows
Ctrl+C or Ctrl+Ins	Copies highlighted stuff to the Clipboard
Ctrl+Esc	Opens the Task List box to show a list of all open applications
Ctrl+Esc, Alt+C	Cascades the windows on the desktop
Ctrl+Esc, Alt+T	Tiles the windows on the desktop
Ctrl+V or Shift+Ins	Pastes stuff from the Clipboard to the active application or window
Ctrl+X or Shift+Del	Cuts highlighted stuff to the Clipboard
Ctrl+Z or Alt+Backspace	The undo key combo
Enter	Used as an 'OK, I'm ready to do this action' key
Esc	Usually gets you out of any sticky situation
Spacebar	Makes a selection in a list box or other area
Tab	Moves you from area to area and from command button to command button in dialog boxes

File Manager Keystrokes	*Results*
F5	Refreshes the directory window view on the current drive
F7	Starts a move
F8	Starts a copy
Ctrl+Down arrow	Shows the next directory at the same level, if one exists, while in the directory tree
Ctrl+Up arrow	Shows the previous directory at the same level, if one exists, while in the directory tree
Home or backslash key	Shows the root directory, while in the directory tree
Left arrow or backspace key	Shows the next directory level up from the current directory, if one exists, while in the directory tree
PgDn	Shows the directory or files (depending on whether you're in the directory tree or directory contents area) one screen down from the current directory, if one exists
PgUp	Shows the directory or files (depending on whether you're in the directory tree or directory contents area) one screen up from the current directory, if one exists
Right arrow	Shows the first subdirectory of the current directory, while in the directory tree
Shift+Enter	Opens a new directory window
Shift+F4	Arranges the directory windows horizontally
Shift+F5	Starts the cascade command
Tab or F6	Moves between the directory tree, the directory contents, and the drive icons
Up or down arrow	Shows the directory above or below the current directory, if one exists, while in the directory tree. If you press a character key, the next directory that begins with that letter or number is selected, while in the directory tree.

Index

Symbols

* wildcard, 110
3 1/2-inch disks, 91
386 Enhanced dialog box, 118-119
  Device Contention: Ports, 118-119
  illustrated, 118
  Minimum Timeslice, 119
  System in Foreground, 119
  Virtual Memory, 119
  Windows in Background, 119
  Windows in Foreground, 119
386 Enhanced icon, 118
  function, 136
386 Enhanced mode, 23, 118-119
  keyboard shortcut, 119
  non-Windows application font
    sizes and, 30
  PIF Editor, 69
  running DOS programs in
    windows and, 66
  running non-Windows applica-
    tions and, 32
>> (greater than symbols), 17
... (ellipsis), 5, 8-9, 17

A

Alt key
  with left/right arrow keys, 16
  See also keyboard shortcuts
application icons, 9
  Clipboard Viewer, 52
  copying, 54
    keyboard shortcut, 56
  deleting, 64
    with groups, 62
  dragging and dropping, 54
  moving, 56
    keyboard shortcut, 56

  rearranging, 49, 50
  See also icons
application windows, 19-21
  arranging, 26-29
  illustrated, 20
  minimizing, 28
  See also document windows;
    windows
applications
  associating files with, 77-79
  non-Windows
    changing font size in, 29-31
    changing settings for running,
      32-34
    running in windows, 34
    starting, 39-40
  quitting, 34-36
  starting, 36-38
    from File Manager, 114-115
    methods for, 38
    non-Windows, 39-40
  switching between, 6, 40-42
  transferring information
    between, 42-45
  Windows and non-Windows, 45
  See also application windows
arrow keys, in File Manager, 80-81
Associate dialog box, 78-79
  Associate With list box, 78, 79
  Browse button, 79
  illustrated, 78

B

Browse dialog box, 79

C

Change Icon dialog box, 61
Chat program, 144
check box, 8

D

Notes

Title	Author	ISBN	Price
DATABASE (continued)			
dBASE For Windows For Dummies™	by Scott Palmer	1-56884-179-5	$19.95 USA/$26.95 Canada
dBASE 5 For Windows Programming For Dummies™	by Ted Coombs & Jason Coombs	1-56884-215-5	$19.99 USA/$26.99 Canada
FoxPro 2.6 For Windows For Dummies™	by John Kaufeld	1-56884-187-6	$19.95 USA/$26.95 Canada
Paradox 5 For Windows For Dummies™	by John Kaufeld	1-56884-185-X	$19.95 USA/$26.95 Canada
DESKTOP PUBLISHING / ILLUSTRATION / GRAPHICS			
CorelDRAW! 5 For Dummies™	by Deke McClelland	1-56884-157-4	$19.95 USA/$26.95 Canada
CorelDRAW! For Dummies™	by Deke McClelland	1-56884-042-X	$19.95 USA/$26.95 Canada
Harvard Graphics 2 For Windows For Dummies™	by Roger C. Parker	1-56884-092-6	$19.95 USA/$26.95 Canada
PageMaker 5 For Macs For Dummies™	by Galen Gruman	1-56884-178-7	$19.95 USA/$26.95 Canada
PageMaker 5 For Windows For Dummies™	by Deke McClelland & Galen Gruman	1-56884-160-4	$19.95 USA/$26.95 Canada
QuarkXPress 3.3 For Dummies™	by Galen Gruman & Barbara Assadi	1-56884-217-1	$19.99 USA/$26.99 Canada
FINANCE / PERSONAL FINANCE / TEST TAKING REFERENCE			
QuickBooks 3 For Dummies™	by Stephen L. Nelson	1-56884-227-9	$19.99 USA/$26.99 Canada
Quicken 8 For DOS For Dummies™, 2nd Edition	by Stephen L. Nelson	1-56884-210-4	$19.95 USA/$26.95 Canada
Quicken 5 For Macs For Dummies™	by Stephen L. Nelson	1-56884-211-2	$19.95 USA/$26.95 Canada
Quicken 4 For Windows For Dummies™, 2nd Edition	by Stephen L. Nelson	1-56884-209-0	$19.95 USA/$26.95 Canada
The SAT I For Dummies™	by Suzee Vlk	1-56884-213-9	$14.95 USA/$20.99 Canada
GROUPWARE / INTEGRATED			
Lotus Notes 3/3.1 For Dummies™	by Paul Freeland & Stephen Londergan	1-56884-212-0$	$19.95 USA/$26.95 Canada
Microsoft Office 4 For Windows For Dummies™	by Roger C. Parker	1-56884-183-3	$19.95 USA/$26.95 Canada
Microsoft Works 3 For Windows For Dummies™	by David C. Kay	1-56884-214-7	$19.99 USA/$26.99 Canada
INTERNET / COMMUNICATIONS / NETWORKING			
CompuServe Starter Kits For Dummies™	by Wallace Wang	1-56884-181-7	$19.95 USA/$26.95 Canada
Modems For Dummies™, 2nd Edition	by Tina Rathbone	1-56884-223-6	$19.99 USA/$26.99 Canada
Modems For Dummies™	by Tina Rathbone	1-56884-001-2	$19.95 USA/$26.95 Canada
MORE Internet For Dummies™	by John R. Levine & Margaret L.Young	1-56884-164-7	$19.95 USA/$26.95 Canada
NetWare For Dummies™	by Ed Tittel & Deni Connor	1-56884-003-9	$19.95 USA/$26.95 Canada
Networking For Dummies™	by Doug Lowe	1-56884-079-9	$19.95 USA/$26.95 Canada
ProComm Plus 2 For Windows For Dummies™	by Wallace Wang	1-56884-219-8	$19.99 USA/$26.99 Canada

12/20/94

Title	Author	ISBN	Price
INTERNET / COMMUNICATIONS / NETWORKING (continued)			
The Internet For Dummies™, 2nd Edition	by John R. Levine & Carol Baroudi	1-56884-222-8	$19.99 USA/$26.99 Canada
The Internet For Macs For Dummies™	by Charles Seiter	1-56884-184-1	$19.95 USA/$26.95 Canada
MACINTOSH			
Macs For Dummies®, 2nd Edition	by David Pogue	1-56884-173-6	$19.95 USA/$26.95 Canada
Macs Programming For Dummies™	by Dan Parks Sydow	1-56884-173-6	$19.95 USA/$26.95 Canada
Macintosh System 7.5 For Dummies™	by Bob LeVitus	1-56884-197-3	$19.95 USA/$26.95 Canada
MORE Macs For Dummies®	by David Pogue	1-56884-087-X	$19.95 USA/$26.95 Canada
PageMaker 5 For Macs For Dummies™	by Galen Gruman	1-56884-178-7	$19.95 USA/$26.95 Canada
QuarkXPress 3.3 For Dummies™	by Galen Gruman & Barbara Assadi	1-56884-217-1	$19.99 USA/$26.99 Canada
Upgrading and Fixing Macs For Dummies™	by Kearney Rietmann & Frank Higgins	1-56884-189-2	$19.95 USA/$26.95 Canada
MULTIMEDIA			
Multimedia & CD-ROMs For Dummies™ Interactive Multimedia Value Pack	by Andy Rathbone	1-56884-225-2	$29.95 USA/$39.95 Canada
Multimedia & CD-ROMs For Dummies™	by Andy Rathbone	1-56884-089-6	$19.95 USA/$26.95 Canada
OPERATING SYSTEMS / DOS			
MORE DOS For Dummies®	by Dan Gookin	1-56884-046-2	$19.95 USA/$26.95 Canada
S.O.S. For DOS™	by Katherine Murray	1-56884-043-8	$12.95 USA/$16.95 Canada
OS/2 For Dummies™	by Andy Rathbone	1-878058-76-2	$19.95 USA/$26.95 Canada
UNIX			
UNIX For Dummies™	by John R. Levine & Margaret Levine Young	1-878058-58-4	$19.95 USA/$26.95 Canada
WINDOWS			
S.O.S. For Windows™	by Katherine Murray	1-56884-045-4	$12.95 USA/$16.95 Canada
MORE Windows "X" For Dummies™, 3rd Edition	by Andy Rathbone	1-56884-240-6	$19.99 USA/$26.99 Canada
PCs / HARDWARE			
Illustrated Computer Dictionary For Dummies™	by Dan Gookin, Wally Wang, & Chris Van Buren	1-56884-004-7	$12.95 USA/$16.95 Canada
Upgrading and Fixing PCs For Dummies™	by Andy Rathbone	1-56884-002-0	$19.95 USA/$26.95 Canada
AutoCAD For Dummies™	by Bud Smith	1-56884-191-4	$19.95 USA/$26.95 Canada
PowerPoint 4 For Windows For Dummies™	by Doug Lowe	1-56884-161-2	$16.95 USA/$22.95 Canada
PRESENTATION / AUTOCAD / PROGRAMMING			
Borland C++ For Dummies™	by Michael Hyman	1-56884-162-0	$19.95 USA/$26.95 Canada
"Borland's New Language Product" For Dummies™	by Neil Rubenking	1-56884-200-7	$19.95 USA/$26.95 Canada

12/20/94

Title	Author	ISBN	Price
PRESENTATION / AUTOCAD / PROGRAMMING (continued)			
C For Dummies™	by Dan Gookin	1-878058-78-9	$19.95 USA/$26.95 Canada
C++ For Dummies™	by Stephen R. Davis	1-56884-163-9	$19.95 USA/$26.95 Canada
Mac Programming For Dummies™	by Dan Parks Sydow	1-56884-173-6	$19.95 USA/$26.95 Canada
QBasic Programming For Dummies™	by Douglas Hergert	1-56884-093-4	$19.95 USA/$26.95 Canada
Visual Basic "X" For Dummies™, 2nd Edition	by Wallace Wang	1-56884-230-9	$19.99 USA/$26.99 Canada
Visual Basic 3 For Dummies™	by Wallace Wang	1-56884-076-4	$19.95 USA/$26.95 Canada
SPREADSHEET			
1-2-3 For Dummies™	by Greg Harvey	1-878058-60-6	$16.95 USA/$21.95 Canada
1-2-3 For Windows 5 For Dummies™, 2nd Edition	by John Walkenbach	1-56884-216-3	$16.95 USA/$21.95 Canada
1-2-3 For Windows For Dummies™	by John Walkenbach	1-56884-052-7	$16.95 USA/$21.95 Canada
Excel 5 For Macs For Dummies™	by Greg Harvey	1-56884-186-8	$19.95 USA/$26.95 Canada
Excel For Dummies™, 2nd Edition	by Greg Harvey	1-56884-050-0	$16.95 USA/$21.95 Canada
MORE Excel 5 For Windows For Dummies™	by Greg Harvey	1-56884-207-4	$19.95 USA/$26.95 Canada
Quattro Pro 6 For Windows For Dummies™	by John Walkenbach	1-56884-174-4	$19.95 USA/$26.95 Canada
Quattro Pro For DOS For Dummies™	by John Walkenbach	1-56884-023-3	$16.95 USA/$21.95 Canada
UTILITIES			
Norton Utilities 8 For Dummies™	by Beth Slick	1-56884-166-3	$19.95 USA/$26.95 Canada
VCRs / CAMCORDERS			
VCRs & Camcorders For Dummies™	by Andy Rathbone & Gordon McComb	1-56884-229-5	$14.99 USA/$20.99 Canada
WORD PROCESSING			
Ami Pro For Dummies™	by Jim Meade	1-56884-049-7	$19.95 USA/$26.95 Canada
MORE Word For Windows 6 For Dummies™	by Doug Lowe	1-56884-165-5	$19.95 USA/$26.95 Canada
MORE WordPerfect 6 For Windows For Dummies™	by Margaret Levine Young & David C. Kay	1-56884-206-6	$19.95 USA/$26.95 Canada
MORE WordPerfect 6 For DOS For Dummies™	by Wallace Wang, edited by Dan Gookin	1-56884-047-0	$19.95 USA/$26.95 Canada
S.O.S. For WordPerfect™	by Katherine Murray	1-56884-053-5	$12.95 USA/$16.95 Canada
Word 6 For Macs For Dummies™	by Dan Gookin	1-56884-190-6	$19.95 USA/$26.95 Canada
Word For Windows 6 For Dummies™	by Dan Gookin	1-56884-075-6	$16.95 USA/$21.95 Canada
Word For Windows For Dummies™	by Dan Gookin	1-878058-86-X	$16.95 USA/$21.95 Canada
WordPerfect 6 For Dummies™	by Dan Gookin	1-878058-77-0	$16.95 USA/$21.95 Canada
WordPerfect For Dummies™	by Dan Gookin	1-878058-52-5	$16.95 USA/$21.95 Canada
WordPerfect For Windows For Dummies™	by Margaret Levine Young & David C. Kay	1-56884-032-2	$16.95 USA/$21.95 Canada

12/20/94

Order Center: **(800) 762-2974** (8 a.m.–6 p.m., EST, weekdays)
*For large quantities call for shipping & handling charges. **Prices are subject to change without notice.

Qty	ISBN	Title	Price	Total

Shipping & Handling Charges

	Description	First book	Each additional book	Total
Domestic	Normal	$4.50	$1.50	$
	Two Day Air	$8.50	$2.50	$
	Overnight	$18.00	$3.00	$
International	Surface	$8.00	$8.00	$
	Airmail	$16.00	$16.00	$
	DHL Air	$17.00	$17.00	$

IDG BOOKS

Please send this order form to:
IDG Books
7260 Shadeland Station
Suite 100
Indianapolis, IN 46256

Allow up to 3 weeks for delivery. Thank you!

Ship to:

Name _____

Company _____

Address _____

City/State/Zip _____

Daytime Phone _____

Payment:

☐ Check to IDG Books (US Funds Only)
☐ VISA
☐ MasterCard
☐ American Express

Card # _____

Exp. _____

Sign. _____

Subtotal _____

CA residents add applicable sales tax_____

IN, MA, and MD residents add 5% sales tax_____

IL residents add 6.25% sales tax_____

RI residents add 7% sales tax_____

TX residents add 8.25% sales tax_____

Shipping_____

Total_____

12/20/94